Tortellini at Midnight

and other heirloom family recipes
from Taranto to Turin to Tuscany

Emiko Davies

Hardie Grant
BOOKS

2

FOREWORD

Tessa Kiros

AUTHOR OF TEN COOKBOOKS INCLUDING
FALLING CLOUDBERRIES* AND *PROVENCE TO PONDICHERRY

My connection with Emiko, who I have gotten to know here in Italy, is that we are both foreigners of mixed heritage living in Tuscany, and are both married to Tuscan men.

We are raising our families within greater, extended families that have strong traditions spanning generations, while also appreciating and celebrating traditions from other parts of the world.

As outsiders, it is not easy to approach a traditional family's cuisine. From our different balconies, we can observe. We can write our stories, then pass them humbly forward. This is our honour.

Over aperitivo, I listened as Emiko spoke of how her husband Marco's great-grandparents had loved and married and journeyed. This truly was a love story: of Nicola, a postman, and Anna, a noblewoman. Their love was a turning point in the history of their families that so easily could have become a different story.

Emiko guides us – with her strong arms – through the streets of this family's journey, from southern to northern, and central Italy. Along the way, Anna and Nicola had nine children, one of who was Mario, Emiko's husband's grandfather.

Anna and Nicola's story was the starting point: the foundation for their future families. Nicola loved Neapolitan songs, while Anna is remembered for her mountains of *polpette* – these became her daughter-in-law Lina's best-foot-forward recipe: the 'exotic' dish she would make when guests came. Lina also took the responsibility of making her own husband, Mario, happy

very seriously, for Mario made all the desserts in the house. He was also a master of preparing quick, tasty meals for himself when he came home late from work, some of which are peppered throughout these pages.

Emiko was unsure of how the real story of Anna's family origin ended. How did they really feel? Did they ever accept her choice of love? But what I really wanted to know at this point in our conversation – by now, I was all-ears – was whether or not they worked out the ingredients in Mario's cake? And, as I listened, I wanted to know what else they would have taken with them from Taranto? I would have loved to have confirmed with them how different their lives must have been after that journey.

These are my favourite kinds of stories. The ones where the family – the people – keep their history and recipes alive and blossoming, and their family roots nourished.

Some people hold the baton and can pass that legacy on. Emiko is, like Nicola was, a messenger, posting stories and recipes for her family to hold and for us to walk side-by-side with.

As we finish talking and I look through the pages of Emiko's book, I am left holding a parcel of thoughts – among them, the chocolate sandwich, the baked oysters, Nonna Anna's *polpette*, *braciolina al burro*, a few truffles. And the urge to travel the length of Italy.

3

CONTENTS

5

6

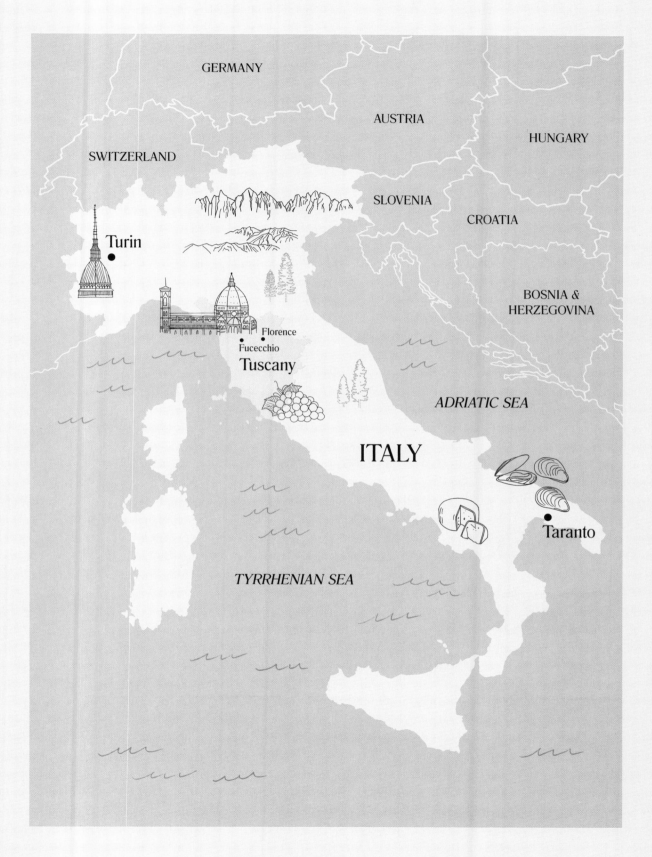

7

(Taranto)
Nicola & Maria
1850–1885   1849–?

(Taranto)
Francesco & Girolama
1849–?   1854–?

(Taranto)
Nicola & Anna
1885–?   1889–1975

(Tuscany)
Angiolino & Maria
1889–1980   1891–1980

(Taranto) (Tuscany)
Mario & Lina
1917–1994   1921–2005

(Tuscany)
Decimo & Vera
1918–2009   1925–

(Tuscany)
Franca & Riccardo
1941–   1939–

(Tuscany)
Angela & Carlo
1946–   1949–2008

(Tuscany) (Australia)
Marco & Emiko
1982–   1980–

INTRODUCTION

'Don't eat anything your great-grandmother
wouldn't recognise as food.'

MICHAEL POLLAN, *IN DEFENSE OF FOOD*, 2008

'Almost everyone in Italy has memories of being
with a grandmother in the kitchen.'

CAROL FIELD, *IN NONNA'S KITCHEN*, 1997

Heirloom recipes tell a story about family through food –
the sort of food that, ironically, doesn't come out of a
cookbook. Many recipes are learned through tasting and
watching, usually from the kitchen table, and through
repetition (and a lot of it, because an unchanging dinner
repertoire is comforting and easy). They are absorbed
through sound, texture and smell – that pathway to
memory – so that, even as adults, some family members
can still recite a recipe that they ate often as a child,
even if they had never cooked it.

Reviving the recipes of past generations is good for
the soul, but it's also simply good; it reflects a time
before processed food – even before refrigeration – when
food was always fresh and nothing went to waste. It's a
way of cooking and eating that relies on the seasons
and what is locally available, and, in the spirit of *cucina
povera*, makes the most of relatively little. It means
cooking and eating together around the table and taking
the time to be with the family.

Here, I have gathered some of the favourite recipes
from our Italian family, tracing back recipes to
generations that span the entire length of Italy, from the
Mediterranean port city of Taranto in the southern heel of
Puglia, to elegant Turin, the city of aperitivo and Italian
café culture in the far north on the border of France and,
finally, back to Tuscany, where we call home.

Mine and my husband Marco's families could not
be more different. I grew up in a multiracial family – a
Japanese mother and an Australian father – in suburban
Australia, before my diplomat father took us back and
forth to China for eight years. My mother, the daughter
of a vegetarian Buddhist priest, made us wonderful
home-cooked meals. During my upbringing in Australia,
she cooked for us every day until we moved to Beijing,
where there was a gentle and friendly cook, Mr Zhang,
who prepared weekday meals for us. I grew up always
loving food; I was an adventurous eater, a keen baker
and was always curious about the kitchen.

Marco, on the other hand, grew up in a small town
in Tuscany, halfway between Florence and Pisa. He
lived with his parents and grandparents under the very
same roof that was built by his great-grandfather. Meals
for the entire family were usually prepared by Marco's
grandmother Lina (decidedly the best cook in the family)
and sometimes by his grandfather Mario (a dapper
Taranto-born, Turin-raised lover of cheese), who dabbled
in desserts, quick dinners and treats, such as fried
mozzarella sandwiches. Until we moved in together,
Marco had never even so much as picked up a wooden
spoon to stir a pot, such was Nonna Lina's long and
beloved reign over the kitchen.

Our kitchen today, in a hilltop neighbourhood
overlooking Florence, is small, but it is the heart of our
home. It's where we play, relax, cook and eat together.
It's where we prepare the food that reminds us of our
grandparents and of trips we have made to Puglia and
Piedmont, and where, together, we eat the dishes that
will become new memories for our daughters.

This is a collection of comforting, family-friendly
recipes and menus that we consider heirlooms to inspire
your own.

FIRST, SECOND, DESSERT

'The pace of an authentically Italian meal is distinctly musical.
The first movement, the pasta or soup, is a *presto agitato*,
fast and eager. The meat is cut, lifted and chewed in a *calmerallegro*,
while the fruit introduces a stately *adagio* of slow, careful selection,
aristocratic discarding, exquisite peeling with knife and fork,
the deliberate, slow jaws returned to serenity.'

KATE SIMON, *ITALY: THE PLACES IN BETWEEN*, 1970

Eating at an Italian table – whether at home or in a restaurant – means following a strict order, one that if disregarded will be met with quizzical looks or perhaps even an eye roll at the cultural blunder committed. The meal starts with antipasto (literally meaning 'before the meal'), a generally small dish that won't ruin your appetite but will complement the dishes to follow. It can often be shared among the table, especially if there's more than one dish. *Primo*, meaning 'first', consists of a course of either pasta, rice or soup. *Secondo* is the main course, usually a meat or fish dish, while *contorni*, simple side dishes of either vegetables or salads, accompany the *secondo*. *Dolce*, dessert, follows. Courses only arrive one at a time, one after the other, not together.

COOK'S NOTES

CHEESE

Pecorino, parmesan, Grana Padano and ricotta salata are interchangeable in most of the dishes where these cheeses are called for; use what you can get or what you have. In general, pecorino (sheep's milk) cheese and ricotta salata are more traditional in Puglia. They are also saltier and have a bit more bite, so keep this in mind when seasoning, and taste the dish often.

COOKING TIMES AND TEMPERATURES

Recipes were tested on a standard gas stovetop. You may need to adjust the heat or cooking times slightly for induction or electric stovetops.

Baking recipes were all baked in a standard conventional oven with an oven thermometer. If you are using a fan-forced or convection oven, you may need to decrease the temperature by 20°C (35°F) or adjust the cooking time.

EGGS

Where possible, use free-range, organic eggs that are approximately 55 g (2 oz), which corresponds to 'large' eggs in the US, Canada and Australia, and 'medium' eggs in Europe.

EQUIPMENT

You don't need any fancy equipment for Italian home cooking, but there are two things that will make life a lot easier: a pasta machine with a crank that attaches to a tabletop and helps roll pasta paper thin, and a *passaverdura*, also known as a *passatutto* or mouli (see page 177), which is a food mill for separating unwanted seeds or skins from sauces and soups. They are not indispensable; you can do the same thing with a rolling pin or a sieve, respectively, but they will help enormously. Many Italians still use a *mezzaluna*: a curved knife for finely chopping vegetables (Nonna Lina always did), but I personally prefer a large, sharp kitchen knife.

GARLIC

Smell an individual garlic clove before using it. It should not smell at all musty or mouldy, but, if it does, immediately discard and try another; that smell is very difficult to hide later. When working with slightly older garlic cloves, in Italy it's common to split the clove in half lengthways and remove the green sprout, if present; Italians believe the sprout makes the garlic difficult to digest.

Some recipes call for a whole garlic, and in our family we like to leave them in (in our house, it's like a prize when you find it on your plate), but you can remove them before serving if you prefer.

MEASUREMENTS

This book uses 20 ml (¾ fl oz) tablespoons; if you are working with 15 ml (½ fl oz) tablespoons, be generous with your tablespoon measurements.

Metric cup measurements are used, i.e. 250 ml (8½ fl oz) for 1 cup; in the US, 1 cup is 237 ml (8 fl oz), so American cooks should be generous with their cup measurements; in the UK, 1 cup is 284 ml (9½ fl oz), so British cooks should be scant with their cup measurements.

MEAT THERMOMETER

Using a meat thermometer is truly the only way to avoid over or undercooking large cuts of meat. Where necessary, I have indicated the internal temperature to aim for when removing meat from a heat source. (Remember that when meat is resting its temperature will continue to rise.)

OLIVE OIL

I only use extra-virgin olive oil for cooking and dressing, except in the case of deep-frying, where a regular olive oil (with a lighter, not-too-fruity flavour) or another vegetable oil should be used.

SALT

I always use sea salt for cooking: fine sea salt for most dishes and coarse sea salt for salting water for pasta. Be aware that using kosher salt or table salt might mean getting different results. In general, table salt is less salty than sea salt and kosher salt can vary in saltiness between brands. I recommend wherever and whenever you can, taste as you go.

SALTING WATER FOR PASTA

Don't skimp on salting pasta cooking water, whether or not the pasta is bland. This is the first thing a Tuscan family will tell you about cooking. To do it correctly, use this formula: 1 teaspoon of sea salt per 1 litre (34 fl oz/4 cups) of water, and approximately 1 litre (34 fl oz/4 cups) of water per 100 g (3½ oz) of dried pasta.

YEAST AND RISING DOUGH

In Italy, fresh yeast is readily available at supermarkets and is more commonly used than dried yeast. As a very simple rule, the less yeast used, the longer the dough will need to rise (overnight, for example, in the refrigerator) and you will be rewarded with a better-developed flavour, better texture and longer-lasting bread. But if you are in a hurry and you only want to let the bread rise for 1 hour (as a minimum), keep it in a warm place to encourage it to rise more quickly. If it's winter and your kitchen is cold, you can even warm up the oven a little, turn it off, then place the bowl in the warmed oven.

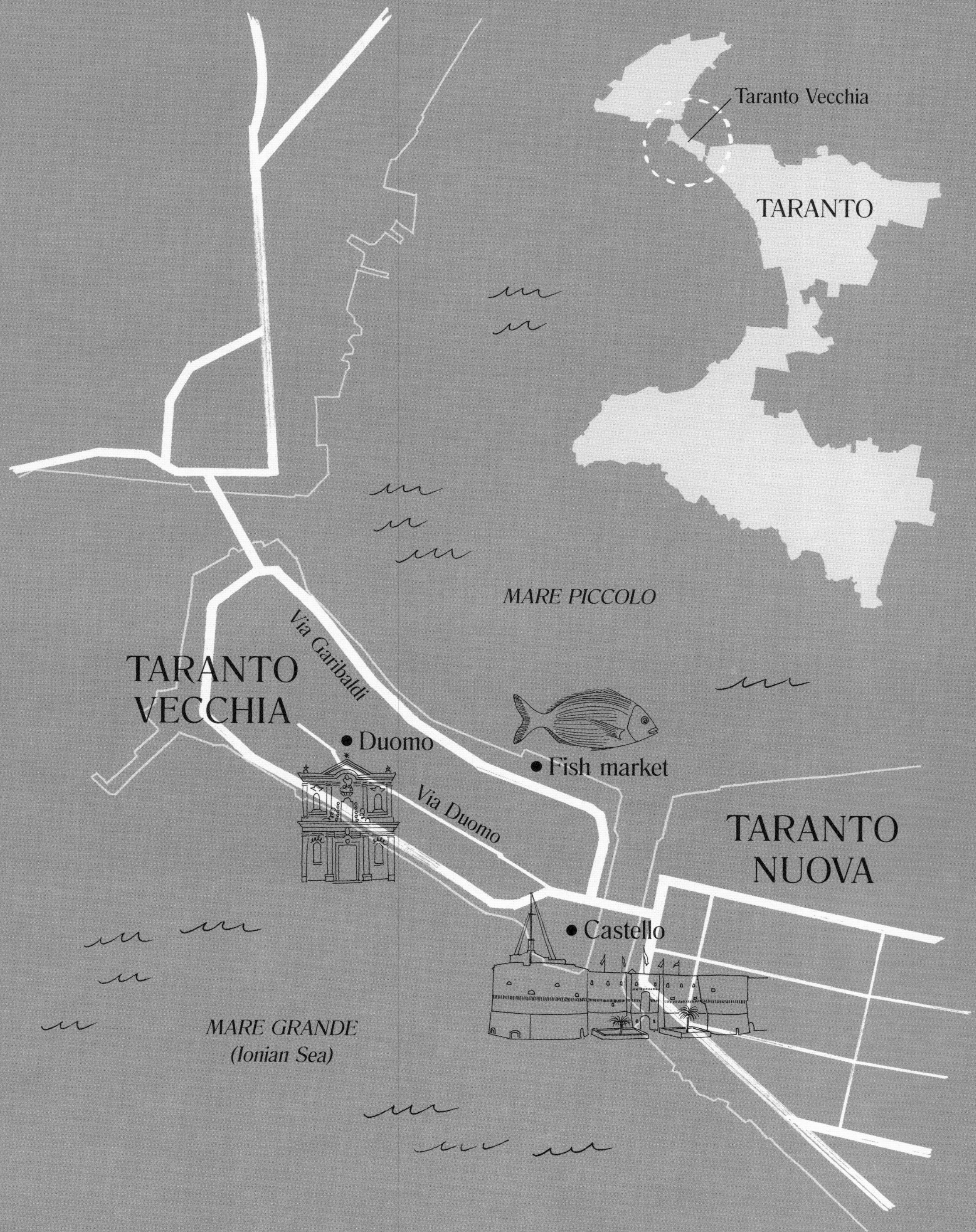

Taranto Vecchia

TARANTO

MARE PICCOLO

TARANTO
VECCHIA

Via Garibaldi

● Duomo

● Fish market

Via Duomo

TARANTO
NUOVA

● Castello

MARE GRANDE
(Ionian Sea)

Taranto

1885

Nicola Cardellicchio was born in a characteristically narrow alleyway of the port city of Taranto, Puglia, in 1885, to a single mother, a widowed wool spinner. While delivering letters, he met and fell in love with Anna, a young noblewoman. Their families' financial differences did not stop them from eloping, even when Anna was disowned. They had nine children in Taranto before moving the family as far north as they could go, to Turin in Piedmont, in search of work after the First World War. Anna may not have learned many dishes to cook as a young woman, but she kept alive in the family a love for *peperoni* (capsicums or bell peppers) and a typical recipe for *polpette* – meatballs in tomato sauce – from her homeland, which her granddaughter Angela, my mother-in-law, still remembers as the dish their Tuscan family made to surprise guests.

20

This page Vico Morrutto, one of the typical dark, narrow streets of Taranto, where Francesco Cardellicchio and Rosa Leone, Nicola's grandfather and grandmother, lived **Opposite page, clockwise from left** A crumbling Taranto street; Taranto's old city; Anna and Nicola with their daughter, Iolanda Cardellicchio

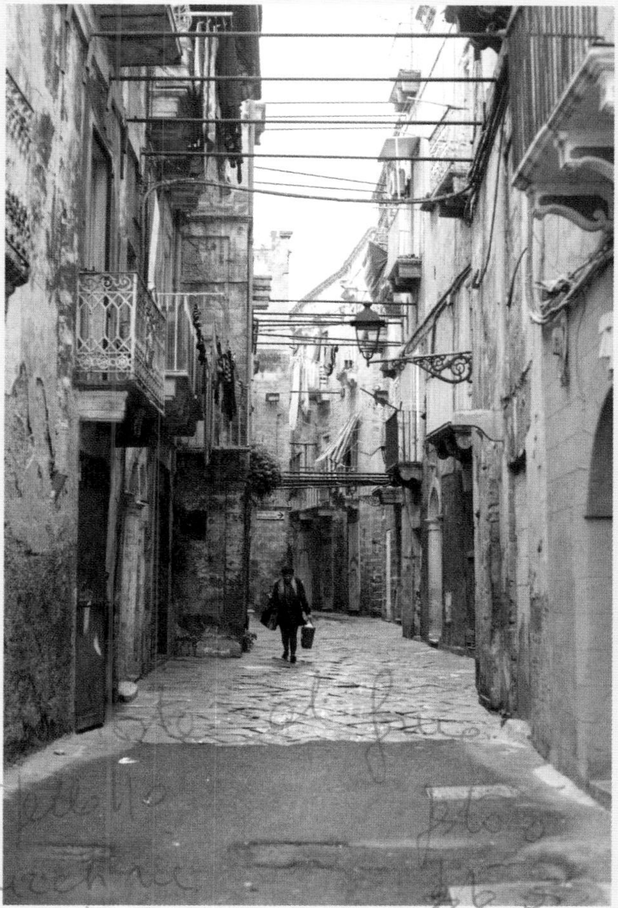

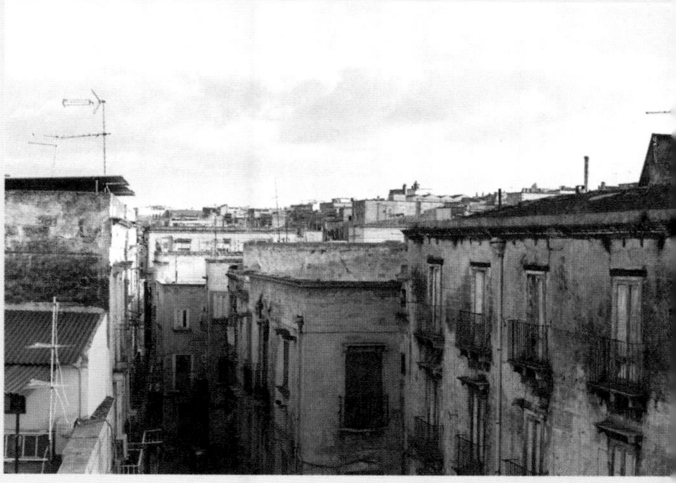

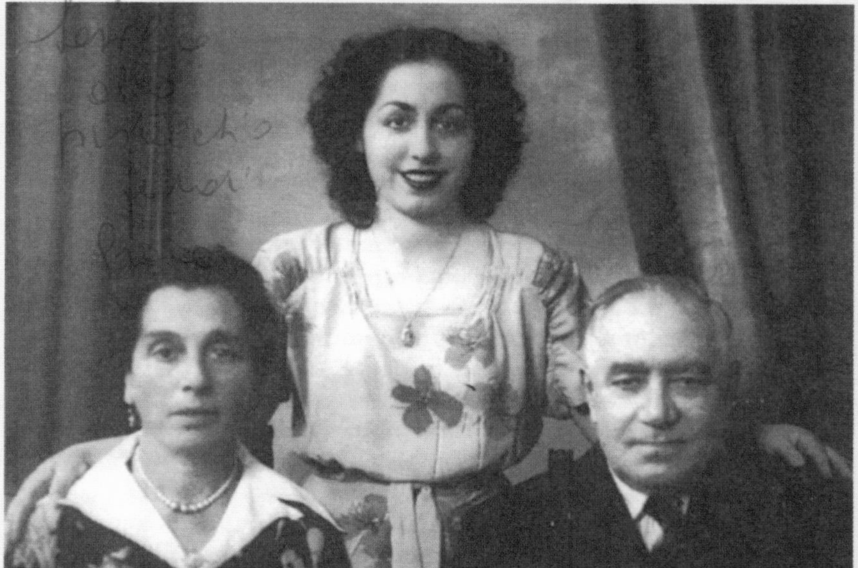

TARANTO, CITY OF TWO SEAS

'Taranto è una città perfetta. Viverci è come vivere nell'interno
di una conchiglia, di un'ostrica aperta. Qui Taranto nuova, là,
gremita, Taranto vecchia, intorno i due mari, e i lungomari.'

(Taranto is a perfect city. Living in it is like living in a shell,
in an open oyster. Here, new Taranto, there, the border,
old Taranto, around them the two seas and the promenades.)

PIER PAOLO PASOLINI, 1959

Taranto is a most curious city. It's geographically split into two. There is the original town, which is referred to as the *borgo antico*, 'the old city' or Taranto *vecchia*, 'old Taranto', a floating island attached to the mainland via two bridges. To the south, you can find the 'new town', Taranto *nuova*, which was developed in the second half of the 1800s with the unification of Italy. To the east of the *borgo antico* is the natural bay known as Mare Piccolo – literally, 'the little sea' – while to the west is the Mare Grande, the Ionian sea.

Its roots are as an ancient (and the only) Greek Spartan colony – *Taras*, it was called, in honour of the son of Poseidon in Greek mythology. The ancient city's coins depict a man (according to mythology, Phalanthos, leader of the Spartans and the founder of Taranto) riding a dolphin – an image that you can find painted on walls throughout the old city as part of the lively street art.

The thing that will strike you most about visiting Taranto's *borgo antico* is probably not the ravaged Greek columns that greet you as you enter Via Duomo, or the fact that it's an island reached by a swing bridge from the new part of town. Instead, it is the crumbling, abandoned buildings, their windows boarded or bricked up, and the walls propped up with metal poles and wood panels. If you look up, sometimes there is a forgotten, glassless window. Cracks reveal, via fallen-in roofs, the colour of the sky. Fig trees and weeds grow

out of strange places – windowsills, rooftops, terraces. Window balconies are missing their floors and the decorative railings are left rusted by the salty sea air.

The British travellers who passed through Taranto from the late 1700s to the early 1900s were all in agreement that the most interesting and beautiful aspect of the old city was its bay, the Mare Piccolo, preferring it to the narrow streets of the city. 'All is strange,' wrote novelist George Gissing of Taranto's old *borgo* in *By the Ionian Sea* (1901), 'but too close-packed to be very striking or beautiful'. He found the marina much more fascinating and commented on the 'admiral figures' of the fishermen with their 'bare legs and arms the tone of terra-cotta[sic],' and noted that their 'lithe limbs, their attitudes at work or in repose, their wild, black hair, perpetually reminded me of shapes pictured on a classic vase'. Meanwhile, in his chapter on Taranto in *Travels in the Two Sicilies* (1783), travel writer Henry Swinburne, visiting Taranto in 1777, describes in great detail the sea life (including a very detailed list of fish in dialect and Latin names), the fishing culture and the Greek history of the city, but describes the ancient, labyrinth-like quarter as 'the most digustful habitation of human beings in Europe, except, perhaps, the Jewish Ghetto in Rome'. He, too, is instead fascinated with the sea and the food he discovers while there, including the grains, the honey, the fruit and, of course, the shellfish.

24

Things don't seem to have changed much since Janet Ross described her first trip to Puglia in her 1889 work *The Land of Manfred*: 'The streets of Taranto are narrow and torturous, particularly near the Marina, now via Garibaldi, where the dirty side alleys seem built for shadows, not men'. At certain times of the day, when every single shop is shut up over long lunch hours, it feels as though you are walking through a graveyard of a city.

Actually, there is life everywhere in the *borgo antico*. On windy days, everyone does their laundry, and sheets and clothes dangle over main streets and alleyways alike. On Sundays, windows and balcony doors are flung open, even on a wintry February morning, and music blasts down the street, echoing off the close buildings. Cats and dogs, collared not strays, take themselves on walks, roaming the streets, sniffing at street corners and opening bags of discarded shells by the garbage bins. Street art decorates the walled-in doors and crumbling eyesores, turning the old town into an open-air art exhibition. And the shrill voices of children playing can be heard everywhere. Small children navigate the narrow alleyways alone, popping into the neighbourhood bar for a treat, playing cards or kicking a soccer ball among the abandoned buildings.

Mozzarella in Carrozza

DEEP-FRIED MOZZARELLA SANDWICHES

Take a bite of this deep-fried mozzarella sandwich, which is said to have been invented in Naples in the 1800s, and you won't be able to think of anything except that string of cheese that gets satisfyingly longer the more you pull the sandwich away from your mouth. It's no wonder that it was called mozzarella in carrozza, literally 'mozzarella in carriage', with the melted mozzarella resembling the reins of a horse and carriage.

While the usual way to make this is to dip the mozzarella sandwiches separately into bowls of flour, beaten egg (with or without milk) and breadcrumbs, I find it works best as described by Tuscan author Edda Servi Machlin in her 1981 cookbook, *The Classic Cuisine of the Italian Jews*. To avoid all the dipping from one dish to the next, she simply combines the egg, milk and flour into a batter – genius, and there's less washing up. I quite like sneaking a few anchovy fillets or slices of ham inside too.

MAKES 4

125 g (4½ oz) fresh mozzarella
125 ml (4 fl oz/½ cup) milk
50 g (1¾ oz/⅓ cup) plain (all-purpose) flour
2 eggs
40 g (1½ oz) dry breadcrumbs
8 thin slices sandwich bread, crusts removed
  (see Note)
125 ml (4 fl oz/½ cup) oil, for frying
  (I like to use olive oil)

Cut the mozzarella into 1 cm (½ in) slices and set aside.

Combine the milk, flour and eggs in a small mixing bowl and whisk with a fork until smooth, then season with salt and pepper. Place the breadcrumbs in a separate small bowl.

Sandwich slices of mozzarella between two slices of bread to make four small sandwiches (if you are making a tray of these for antipasto, for example, you can cut them in half for smaller triangles). Dip the edges of each sandwich into the batter, then dip in the breadcrumbs to seal the edges. Now dip the entire sandwich in the batter until fully coated and place on a large tray, board or plate and repeat with the remaining sandwiches. Press the edges of the sandwiches together slightly.

Pour the oil into a wide, heavy-based pan (I prefer cast iron for frying) to a depth of 2 cm (¾ in). Place over a medium heat and heat gently to 160°C (320°F), or until a cube of bread dropped into the oil turns golden brown in 15 seconds. You want to fry the sandwiches relatively slowly so that the cheese has time to melt.

Working in batches to avoid overcrowding, place the sandwiches in a single layer in the pan and fry until evenly golden brown, about 2 minutes on each side. Flip the sandwiches over carefully and, if needed, turn the sandwiches on their edges using a pair of tongs and fry until crisp. Remove from the oil and drain on paper towels or place on a wire rack. Season immediately with a sprinkle of salt.

Usually good fried snacks need to be served piping hot, right out of the pan, but these sandwiches work surprisingly well when reheated in the oven – handy if you need to prepare these ahead of time. Allow the sandwiches to cool completely on a wire rack, wrap well in plastic wrap or store in an airtight container in the fridge and, when ready to serve, place the sandwiches on a baking tray and simply reheat in a 180°C (350°F) oven until piping hot.

29

NOTE

*This dish was invented to make good use of
leftovers – bread that was perhaps going stale,
and not-so-fresh mozzarella that was tastier when
cooked. Today, it is commonly made with soft,
white sandwich bread, which easily squashes
so you can seal the edges, but it is infinitely
tastier when you use a delicious sourdough bread
or country-style, wood-fired bread such as a
traditional Italian bread. The sealing of the edges
is quite an important part of the success of this
delicious snack, and there are many other ways
to ensure the precious filling doesn't escape
during cooking, including dipping just the edges
in breadcrumbs, double dipping or, especially
good if you're using a firmer bread, soaking the
bread in egg first for 30 minutes to soften it (this
is a tip from Elizabeth David). Finally, consider
using fresh buffalo mozzarella; the milky liquid
that seeps out of fresh mozzarella will help hold
the sandwich together.*

30

Panzerotti

FRIED CHEESE AND TOMATO PASTRIES

A *panzerotto* (*panzerotti* is plural) is essentially a small, deep-fried calzone: pizza dough harbouring a filling of mozzarella and tomato sauce in its most classic form. They are, along with *Pucce* (see pages 35–6), one of Taranto's most iconic street snacks or lunches on the run. There is something magical about fried pizza dough – it is golden and incredibly crisp on the outside, impossibly fluffy on the inside and it stays hot for a long time (take note, impatient, hungry eaters).

Around town, the places specialising in *panzerotti* will have long lists of enticing fillings just as in a pizzeria, but the *semplice*, or the classic, filling is mozzarella and tomato sauce, followed closely by the addition of ham or mortadella. This recipe sounds like it makes a large quantity, but it's worth it as these *panzerotti* freeze very well if you're not using them all at once and, if you are, they make perfect party fare.

32

MAKES ABOUT 16 PANZEROTTI

vegetable oil, for frying

DOUGH

10 g (¼ oz) fresh yeast or 3 g
   (just over 1 teaspoon) active dry yeast
125 ml (4 fl oz/½ cup) lukewarm water
500 g (1 lb 2 oz) plain (all-purpose) flour,
   plus extra for dusting
125 ml (4 fl oz/½ cup) milk
60 ml (2 fl oz/¼ cup) olive oil, plus extra
   for oiling
1½ teaspoons salt

FILLING

250 g (9 oz) tomato passata (puréed tomatoes)
500 g (1 lb 2 oz) fresh mozzarella

Prepare the dough by combining the yeast and water and leaving to soften for 5–10 minutes. Sift the flour into a large, wide mixing bowl and add the yeast mixture, milk, olive oil and salt, and mix until combined into a dough. Knead on a lightly floured surface (it may be somewhat sticky at first) for about 7–10 minutes, or until you have a smooth, elastic ball of dough. Lightly oil the bowl and place the dough back inside, cover tightly with plastic wrap or place a slightly damp tea towel (dish towel) over the top. Leave to sit in a warm corner of the kitchen (free from draughts)

to rise for 2 hours (3 if your kitchen is cold), or until the dough has doubled in size. Alternatively, place the bowl in the fridge and let the dough rise slowly for 8–12 hours, or overnight.

While the dough is rising, prepare the filling. Season the passata with salt and pepper, and heat gently over a low heat in a small saucepan. Bring to a simmer and cook for 10 minutes, then set aside to cool.

Cut the mozzarella into small dice and place in a fine-mesh sieve set over a bowl to drain out the whey. Set aside in the fridge.

When the dough has risen, portion it into sixteen balls, roughly 50 g (1¾ oz) each. Place the balls on a baking tray or a chopping board lined with baking paper and leave to rise for another hour. Loosely cover with a slightly damp tea towel so they do not dry out.

On a lightly floured surface, roll out each ball of dough to a thin circle, about 1–2 mm (¹⁄₁₆ in) thick. Place half a tablespoon of passata and about 1 tablespoon of mozzarella in the centre of each circle. Fold in half and press the edges down firmly, then fold over the edge again by about 1 cm (½ in) to double seal (you'll be in trouble if the panzerotti come undone during frying). Repeat with the remaining balls of dough.

If you're not cooking them right away, at this point you can leave them in the fridge (in a single layer on a tray lined with baking paper so they do not stick) for an hour or two before frying (bring them to room temperature 30 minutes before frying). Otherwise, freeze them, as above, in a single layer on a tray. Once frozen hard, transfer them to freezer bags to freeze for up to 3 months. Fry from frozen until evenly golden brown.

To fry, heat enough vegetable oil in a saucepan to cover the panzerotti completely (at least 5 cm/2 in) over a medium heat. It is ready when it has reached 160°C (320°F) on a cooking thermometer. If you don't have a thermometer, drop a cube of white bread into the oil. It should turn golden brown in 15 seconds. If it colours too quickly, turn the heat down slightly. Fry the panzerotti in batches for 2–3 minutes, or until golden brown and puffed all over.

Pucce con gli Uccelletti

PIZZA SANDWICHES WITH PANCETTA-WRAPPED SCAMORZA

Pucce (or *puccia*, singular) are, along with *panzerotti*, another of Taranto's iconic street foods and, although a version of the *puccia* exists in Salento in Puglia's south, Tarantini will hotly contest that real *puccia* belongs to them. It is nothing more than plain pizza dough, cooked in a smaller size, preferably in a wood-fired oven. The resulting flat round of hot bread is then sliced open and stuffed with favourite hot or cold fillings like a panino – it may be as simple as some *salame* and cheese, or perhaps tinned tuna, tomato and rocket (arugula), but a unique filling that you'll find only in Taranto is *uccelletti* (literally 'little birds'), consisting of small balls of smoked scamorza wrapped in thin slices of speck or pancetta. They're roasted in the same oven as the *pucce* until simultaneously crisp (the pancetta) and melted (the cheesy interior). In Taranto's many *puccerie*, *uccelletti* are famously paired with an impossible amount of french fries, but I prefer them with a fresh rocket salad and chopped tomatoes.

You can make *pucce* ahead of time and fill them later (they're still good even the next day), but there is no doubt that, like pizza, these are at their absolute best fresh out of the oven and still hot. You can easily halve this recipe, but I think it's worth making the whole lot as you can freeze half of the dough for later. Let the dough rise fully, then double wrap each portion separately in plastic wrap. When you want to use it, thaw it in the fridge overnight or on the kitchen bench for two hours; in either case, let the dough come to room temperature before using as normal.

35

MAKES 4 PUCCE

handful of rocket (arugula)
2 ripe tomatoes, diced
drizzle of extra-virgin olive oil

PUCCE DOUGH

20 g (¾ oz) fresh yeast or 7 g (2½ level
    teaspoons) active dry yeast
250 ml (8½ fl oz/1 cup) lukewarm water
500 g (1 lb 2 oz) plain (all-purpose) flour,
    plus extra for dusting
60 ml (2 fl oz/¼ cup) extra-virgin olive oil
1½ teaspoons salt

UCCELLETTI

16 *scamorzine* (small balls of scamorza)
    or mozzarella (approx. 400 g/14 oz; see Note)
16 paper-thin slices pancetta
    (approx. 120 g/4½ oz)

For the dough, crumble or stir the yeast into about half of the water in a large mixing bowl and leave to soften for 5–10 minutes. Sift the flour into the bowl and add the rest of the water, the olive oil and salt, and mix well to create a dough. Knead the dough on a lightly floured surface (it may be somewhat sticky at first) for about 7–10 minutes, or until you have a smooth, elastic ball of dough.

Lightly oil the bowl and place the dough back inside, cover tightly with plastic wrap or place a slightly damp tea towel (dish towel) over the top. Leave to sit in a warm corner of the kitchen (free from draughts) to rise for 2 hours (3 if your kitchen is cold), or until the dough has doubled in size. Alternatively, place the bowl in the fridge and let the dough rise slowly for 8–12 hours, or overnight.

Divide the dough into four even portions (having wet hands will help when handling the dough). Roll the blobs of dough lightly in flour, then flatten them directly onto a baking sheet (lined with baking paper if necessary) or a pizza stone. They should be about 15 cm (6 in) in diameter. Cover with a tea towel and leave to rise/rest for a further 30 minutes. In the meantime, heat the oven to 200°C (400°F). Bake the pucce for 15 minutes.

To prepare the uccelletti, simply wrap the small balls of scamorza in the slices of pancetta and place in a baking dish. Bake in the same oven as the pucce (if you have space) for 15 minutes, or until the cheese is melted and the pancetta looks golden brown. Otherwise, bake the pucce first and leave them whole, then bake the uccelletti (note that if you are using mozzarella instead of scamorzine, you may not need to bake them for the full 15 minutes).

To serve, slice the pucce open and divide the baked uccelletti between each, along with some fresh rocket and diced tomato. The uccelletti are flavourful enough, but I like to season the tomato and salad with some extra-virgin olive oil and freshly ground black pepper.

NOTE

If you can't find small balls of smoked scamorza, you can use a large ball and cut it into pieces. Alternatively, small balls of mozzarella work well too, even if they are a bit creamier and melt faster. You can also use speck (a dry-cured and smoked ham) instead of the pancetta if you're using mozzarella so that you get that smoky flavour you would normally have with the scamorza, but I find a scamorza-speck combination all a bit too smoky.

Ostriche Arraganate

BAKED OYSTERS

'Oysters are excellent and cheap; it is worth a journey
to Taranto to sail on the Mare Piccolo and haul up the
long strands of rope, choosing one's oyster as they
come dripping out of the sea.'

JANET ROSS, *THE LAND OF MANFRED*, 1889

Taranto's inner bay, the Mare Piccolo, has the rather unique feature of numerous *citri*, natural freshwater springs, that create an environment of brackish water – it is the perfect place for cultivating bivalves. As a result, shellfish in Taranto are cheap, plentiful and, because they are also exceptionally tasty, they are almost always consumed raw. But there are, naturally, countless recipes for preparing the beloved shellfish in other ways, and this incredibly simple dish is one I particularly love (this, coming from someone who had previously thought that oysters have no place being cooked).

Everyone puts their own stamp on this classic preparation for *oscre arrustute*, as they are known in Taranto's dialect. Some may add to this basic recipe some oregano, finely chopped garlic, a sprinkle of pecorino, grated caciocavallo or lemon juice, but I find these additions (in particular the cheeses) superfluous, especially if you want the flavour of the oysters to shine through.

This dish would typically be part of antipasto (in Taranto's fish restaurants, they often cook mussels this way too, served alongside four or five other small cooked seafood dishes), but it also makes a delicious light lunch for two with a bright salad of peppery rocket (arugula) or other green salad, dressed simply with lemon juice and extra-virgin olive oil.

SERVES 4 AS ANTIPASTO

1 kg (2 lb 3 oz) freshly shucked oysters
    (about 8 if very large)
2–3 tablespoons very finely chopped flat-leaf
    (Italian) parsley
30 g (1 oz) dry breadcrumbs
80 ml (2½ fl oz/⅓ cup) extra-virgin olive oil

Preheat the oven to 200°C (400°F).

Drain any water off the oysters by tipping them gently. Place the oysters on a baking tray and evenly sprinkle them first with the parsley, followed by the breadcrumbs, then the olive oil and plenty of freshly ground black pepper. You won't need any salt for this; oysters are tasty enough.

Bake in the hot oven for 10 minutes, or until the breadcrumbs are crisp and lightly golden. Serve immediately.

38

Acciughe al Forno con Burrata

FRESH ANCHOVIES BAKED WITH BURRATA

In my mind, this is the coming together of two of the best things in the world: fried anchovies and creamy, oozing burrata from Puglia. It may seem, at first, a shame to cook burrata when it is so incredibly good fresh, but this makes such a delicious meal, with the burrata melting into a creamy filling for the fried anchovies, that you won't regret baking it. This is the kind of effortless dish I love to cook for friends as part of a bigger feast. It's usually served in smaller portions as part of antipasto but, like the *Ostriche arraganate* (page 38), you could easily serve this as a light lunch for two or three, along with a crunchy and zingy salad.

In Italy, fishmongers often sell anchovies completely whole, to be taken home and cleaned and butterflied yourself. If your fishmonger hasn't done them for you, see the first paragraph of the recipe, otherwise you can also purchase ready-butterflied fresh anchovies and start from the third paragraph.

SERVES 4 AS ANTIPASTO

400 g (14 oz) whole fresh anchovies (approx.
  250 g/9 oz cleaned, butterflied anchovies)
50 g (1¾ oz/⅓ cup) plain (all-purpose) flour
60 ml (2 fl oz/¼ cup) extra-virgin olive oil,
  plus extra for drizzling
20 g (¾ oz) pecorino, grated
20 g (¾ oz) dry breadcrumbs
small handful of basil and/or flat-leaf (Italian)
  parsley, finely chopped
250 g (9 oz) fresh burrata

To clean whole anchovies, snap off the head from the bottom up towards the spinal cord. Run the nail of your thumb lengthways along the belly to open (alternatively you can use a small, sharp knife) and simultaneously remove the guts, which should come away easily. Running water from the sink can be handy to wash this away, though it's not entirely necessary as you can rinse the fish later, then drain on paper towels.

Continue running the nail of your thumb down the whole length of the body of the fish to split it in two, lengthways, and open it like a book. The spinal cord should now be exposed. Pull it out, starting from the head end and snapping it off at

the tail. Once you get the hang of this, you can do all of this in one swift motion – and head, spine and entrails all come out in a clean, easy sweep.

Place the flour in a small bowl and dip the filleted anchovies in the flour to lightly coat. Heat the olive oil in a small saucepan over a medium heat and shallow-fry the anchovy fillets for about 1 minute on each side, or until golden. You may need to do this in two batches: first using half of the olive oil, then cleaning the pan before adding the remaining olive oil for the second batch. Drain the fried anchovies on paper towels.

Combine the pecorino, breadcrumbs and herbs in a small bowl. Preheat the oven to 180°C (350°F).

In a small baking dish (about 15 x 23 cm/ 6 x 9 in), arrange half of the fried anchovies in a single layer, sprinkle with salt and pepper, then tear over half of the burrata. Repeat with the remaining anchovies in another layer, followed by another sprinkle of salt and pepper, finishing with the burrata and covering with the pecorino mixture. Drizzle over a little olive oil.

Bake for 15–20 minutes, or until the top is golden brown and bubbling.

Scamorza alla Pizzaiola

SCAMORZA IN TOMATO SAUCE

This is a dish that Marco's grandfather, Nonno Mario, would make for himself when he came home late from work on the train from Florence and had missed lunch completely. Mario never had a name for it, it was just a happy coincidence of delicious things brought together in a pan for a quick meal, but I found that many families had something similar in their household with various names (and cheeses, usually mozzarella): *pizza pazza* or 'crazy pizza', *pizza povera* or 'poor pizza', *mozzarella al padellino* or 'mozzarella in a pan' and *alla pizzaiola* – 'pizza style'. This last one seemed to make the most sense to me and it is very similar to other dishes *alla pizzaiola*, such as the scaloppine on page 213.

If you don't have scamorza – a wonderful, pear-shaped cheese, which comes in smoked or milder *dolce* varieties and has a firm consistency that is excellent for melting – you can use provolone, caciocavallo, or fresh fior di latte or buffalo mozzarella – really, any other good melting cheese that you have to hand. Note that mozzarella is sweeter and milder than the other full-flavoured cheeses mentioned, so do keep this in mind when seasoning the sauce.

SERVES 4

2–3 tablespoons extra-virgin olive oil,
   plus extra for drizzling
1 garlic clove
500 g (1 lb 2 oz) tomato passata (puréed
   tomatoes) or tinned chopped tomatoes
300 g (10½ oz) scamorza
   (about 2 fist-sized balls)
fresh basil or oregano leaves
4 slices good crusty bread (toasted is best)

Heat the olive oil in a wide, deep pan over a low heat, add the garlic clove and gently sizzle. Be careful it doesn't burn; you simply want to infuse the oil with the garlic for a minute or two, or until you can detect the fragrance of garlic wafting up from the pan.

Pour in the passata and season with salt and pepper. Add a splash of water (if you're using fresh mozzarella instead of scamorza, the cheese will release plenty of liquid so you may not need the extra water and, instead, you may want to reduce the sauce a little more than what follows).

Let the sauce simmer rapidly over a medium heat for about 10 minutes, or until thickened and reduced slightly. Taste for seasoning.

Cut the scamorza into 1 cm (½ in) thick slices and lay them over the sauce in a single layer, if possible. Without touching the pan's contents, continue simmering for a further 5 minutes or until the cheese is perfectly melted (if you find the sauce is reducing more than you would like but the cheese is not yet melted to perfection, take the pan off the heat and let it sit, covered, for about 5 minutes).

Give the cheese one quick stir to distribute evenly through the sauce – this is the way it has always been done in our household, but some may prefer to leave the cheese slices 'whole' and relatively separate from the sauce. Serve with whole basil leaves on top and either pour the sauce over the toasted bread or serve the dish in a shallow bowl with bread on the side to dip into the sauce. More ground pepper and an extra drizzle of olive oil are optional but much loved in our family.

Fagiolini Sfiziosi

GREEN BEANS DRESSED IN BREADCRUMBS

Fagiolini sfiziosi, or *fagiulini spilusieddi* in dialect, can be translated as beans that are either appetising, satiating, frivolous or fanciful – or perhaps all of these things. I came across this simple side dish bursting with fresh flavours during my very first visit to Puglia one early summer. As we drove from one end of Puglia to the other, I was enthralled at the sight of field after field of luscious vegetable patches growing in deep-red soil, not to mention the produce markets and menus showcasing plentiful and cheap sun-ripened vegetables, including things I had never seen before. Finally, I understood exactly why Puglia is often referred to as the vegetable patch of Italy.

This is a great side dish to prepare for a barbecue or a picnic as you can make it in advance and, when the flavours have had time to get to know each other, it's all the better for it.

44

SERVES 4

400 g (14 oz) green beans
　(string or round beans)
3 tablespoons extra-virgin olive oil,
　plus extra for drizzling
4 spring onions (scallions), white part only,
　thinly sliced
20 g (¾ oz) dry breadcrumbs
handful of flat-leaf (Italian) parsley leaves,
　chopped
handful of mint leaves, chopped or torn
juice of 1 lemon

Rinse, dry and cut off the tops of the beans (if they are very long, you can cut them in half too). Bring a saucepan of salted water to the boil and cook the beans for a few minutes, or until they are still bright green and 'al dente' or with a slight bite to them. In the meantime, prepare a bowl full of iced water. Drain the beans, then immediately transfer them to the iced water to cool them down quickly and stop the cooking process. Set aside to dry on clean tea towels (dish towels).

Meanwhile, heat the oil in a pan over a low–medium heat and cook the sliced spring onions until softened and slightly golden. Add the breadcrumbs, season with salt and pepper, and continue cooking for a few minutes, or until the crumbs are golden and crisp, then remove from the heat.

In a bowl, toss together the drained beans, the breadcrumb mixture, herbs, lemon juice and an extra drizzle of olive oil. You can serve this dish immediately while warm, but I also like it at room temperature.

Peperoni Arrostiti

GRILLED CAPSICUMS

This features often in ours and my in-laws' households, especially in the summer and when grilled *bistecca* (Florentine style T-bone steak) is on the menu. We almost always use yellow capsicum (bell pepper), occasionally red but never green (green capsicums are the least ripe so they are less sweet and slightly more bitter; red peppers are the sweetest and yellow are the 'just right' peppers for this, falling wonderfully in between). The scent of peppers roasting, their skins blistering black, rises through the house and is one of those things that triggers in Marco memories of childhood summers and of his Nonna Lina, who would prepare this dish for every single Sunday dinner throughout the summer. Lina's version, like the traditional Pugliese version that she was taught by her mother-in-law, had thin slices of raw garlic in it too.

The Italian verb *arrostire* means to roast, but it also means to cook over a live fire, which is the best way to prepare these peppers, as they take on extra flavour when they come in contact with the fire. If you're already grilling meat such as a *bistecca* over the fire, it makes sense to use the same method to cook these whole peppers, perhaps at that point when the fire is too hot and the flames too high for the *bistecca*, which fares better over hot coals. If you don't have a fireplace (or don't fancy lighting it during a sweltering Italian summer), you can also cook these over a barbecue outdoors or directly on the gas hob.

SERVES 4

2 large yellow capsicums (bell peppers), approx. 800 g/1 lb 12 oz
1–2 tablespoons extra-virgin olive oil
1–2 tablespoons red-wine vinegar
mint or basil leaves, to serve (optional)

Rinse and dry the capsicums and keep them perfectly whole. Blacken the skins of the capsicums evenly by placing directly over the flames of a fire, barbecue or gas hob (place the peppers directly on the hobs over a high heat) and turn carefully and regularly with a pair of long tongs for about 20 minutes. You want to make sure you get the skins of the peppers completely and entirely roasted black. Sometimes you may have to hold the vegetable with tongs directly over the flame to roast the hard-to-reach spots.

Once blackened, place the hot capsicums in a bowl and cover tightly with plastic wrap, or pop them in a zip-lock bag and leave them to sweat for 10 minutes or so, or until cool enough to handle.

Remove the skin (all traces of it). I find this easiest under a gentle, steady stream of cool water from the tap. While there, pull out the stem and the seeds and open up the capsicums. Once peeled and cleaned of seeds, pat dry with paper towels and cut or tear into long strips. Place in a bowl and dress with olive oil, vinegar and salt and pepper to taste, tossing everything together to coat evenly.

Serve warm, cool or at room temperature. These keep very well for several days in an airtight container in the fridge (the flavours just seem to get better the longer you leave them to linger). Just before serving, you can add some fresh mint or basil leaves, if you like.

ON PEPERONI

Peperoni, or capsicums or bell peppers, are not native to Italy, even though they have become a symbol of the cuisine, particularly in southern Italy. Like tomatoes, capsicums were one of the many things brought to the Old World after Christopher Columbus stumbled upon the Americas in 1492. And, like tomatoes, capsicums were not initially considered edible. Recipes for capsicums first appear in the seventeenth-century cookbooks written by Carlo Nascia, the Sicilian chef to the Farnese dukes, as well as that of the head steward to the king of Naples, Antonio Latini (who, Elizabeth David notes in *Italian Food*, also penned the oldest-known recipe for tomato sauce in his *Lo Scalco alla Moderno*).

Today in Italy, *peperoni* are guaranteed all over and all year round in supermarkets, even if they are decidedly sweeter and better in the summer season. But my mother-in-law, Angela, remembers in her youth finding them sporadically in the market of her small Tuscan town and only ever in the summer – and, even then, it was still rare for Tuscans to be familiar with them. Even later on, in the 1980s, Angela prepared roasted peppers for a lunch conference in Pisa and not one person dared try the unfamiliar dish. Because of her father and her grandmother's southern Italian heritage, their family would buy them whenever they were in season and she too grew up eating capsicums, especially stuffed with meat (see pages 86–7) – a dish that her mother Lina was taught by Nonna Anna – or roasted on the flames of an open fire (see page 47).

I find it interesting that *peperoni* don't have much to do with Tuscan cooking at all. A look at some of the classic cookbooks that cover the region produces very few results: Paolo Petroni's colossal *Il Libro della Vera Cucina Toscana* of more than 1000 Tuscan recipes contains just one with capsicums. Pellegrino Artusi's *Science in the Kitchen and the Art of Eating Well* – which was printed in 1891 while Artusi lived in Florence, contains 790 recipes and is considered the bible of Italian cuisine – has one recipe too, for a *salsa di peperoni*: a sauce made with green capsicums.

While capsicums are very much associated with southern Italian cooking – where they are practically a staple of the kitchen – you can also find them in the seemingly unlikely far north, in Piedmont. You can even find a variety of capsicum known as *peperoni di Carmagnola* grown in the provinces of Turin and Cuneo. Introduced in the nineteenth century, capsicums have become a vital and integral part of the economy and food culture in the area to the point where they are omnipresent. In Turin, you'll be hard pressed to find a classic restaurant or café that doesn't offer capsicum in some form – cooked with anchovies as antipasto, raw for dipping in a warm, garlicky sauce of *Bagna cauda* (page 119), or even sandwiched in a *Tramezzino* (pages 116–7) – and, in late summer, you can visit Carmagnola (along with another quarter of a million visitors), just outside of Turin, for their *sagra del peperone*, an annual fair dedicated to their precious capsicums.

48

Parmigiana di Melanzane

EGGPLANT PARMIGIANA

Parmigiana is a layered vegetable dish that has nothing to do with parmesan cheese or the northern Italian town of Parma (as it is often mistakenly thought), and everything to do with southern Italian cooking. It has all the hallmarks of a true icon of Italian cuisine; it is resourceful, seasonal, economic and deliciously satisfying all at once.

Nonna Lina used to prepare this in the summer. It is a dish she learned from her Pugliese mother-in-law, Anna. Like *peperoni*, eggplants (aubergines) were not always commonplace in Tuscan markets and as well known and popular as Parmigiana is today all over Italy (and indeed worldwide). In fact, not long ago, it was still relatively unknown. Angela, my own mother-in-law, remembers bringing a tray of Parmigiana to a picnic with friends in the early 1970s and not one of her large group of Tuscan friends had ever heard of or tasted such a dish.

I always think of Parmigiana as a *piatto unico*: a dish that isn't a *primo* or a *secondo*, but is basically hearty enough that it covers the entire meal (especially if, like some, you add to it mortadella, sausage or a couple of eggs, beaten and poured over the top to form a lovely golden crust – this last one was an addition Lina always made). But in Puglia, Parmigiana is considered an antipasto, and, indeed, if you serve it in small enough portions, you could get away with eating this as a starter or even a side dish. But when we make Parmigiana, this is all we eat, along with a bright and simple salad of greens.

51

SERVES 4
AS A MAIN OR 6 AS ANTIPASTO

2 large eggplants (aubergines)
(approx. 1 kg/2 lb 3 oz)
2 tablespoons extra-virgin olive oil
1 small onion, finely chopped
500 g (1 lb 2 oz) tomato passata (puréed
tomatoes)
handful of fresh basil leaves
500 ml (17 fl oz/2 cups) vegetable oil, for frying
1 large ball (approx. 200 g/7 oz) fresh
mozzarella, sliced
80 g (2¾ oz) aged pecorino
(or parmesan or caciocavallo), grated

Peel the eggplants if you like, then cut them lengthways into 1 cm (½ in) thick slices. Layer them in a colander and sprinkle each layer generously with salt (don't worry, you will rinse it off later). Finish layering and salting the slices, then place a plate on top followed by a weight (such as a tin of beans or tomatoes). Leave for a minimum of 30 minutes and up to 1 hour. During this time, the eggplant slices will weep a brownish liquid. Rinse them under cold water and carefully pat them dry with clean tea towels (dish towels).

While the eggplants are draining, prepare the tomato sauce by heating the olive oil in a deep pan over a low heat. Add the onion and cook gently until soft and translucent but not coloured, about 10 minutes. Add the passata, along with a few basil leaves, a splash of water and a pinch of salt (try not to salt this sauce too much; it should be bright and fresh – also keep in mind the cheese, especially if using caciocavallo, which will add some saltiness too). Increase the heat to medium and leave to simmer for 15 minutes, or until the sauce is as thick as you like it. Set aside until needed.

Pour the vegetable oil into a wide saucepan, preferably one that will fit three or four eggplant slices at a time. Set over a medium–high heat. The oil is hot enough when a cube of eggplant dropped into the oil sizzles immediately. Fry three or four slices at a time, a few minutes on each side, or until they are evenly golden brown. Drain well on paper towels and leave to cool. Change the paper towels as necessary and continue frying until all the slices are cooked.

Preheat the oven to 180°C (350°F).

Assemble the Parmigiana by first spooning some tomato sauce in a thin layer over the bottom of a rectangular or oval ceramic or glass casserole dish (ideally, the kind that you can also present at the table). Top with a single layer of eggplant, then spoon over some more tomato sauce, a few torn up basil leaves and a handful of cheese – both mozzarella and pecorino. Continue layering eggplant, tomato sauce and basil, ending with a more generous layer of cheese, in particular the pecorino. Bake for 25–30 minutes, or until you can see the edges bubbling and a golden-brown crust has formed. It's best to let the Parmigiana sit for about 15–20 minutes before cutting into it, and it's also delicious served tepid rather than piping hot – a real treat on a hot summer's night.

NOTE

How the eggplants are treated is probably the most important part of a successful Parmigiana. Those who shy away from deep-frying usually go for grilling the eggplants, but this is neither traditional nor the best way to prepare eggplants for this particular dish. Deep-frying is the preferred method of purists for a good reason: fried, the eggplant slices give way to an utterly silky, almost melting texture. But some go a step further, first dusting with flour, dipping in egg and then deep-frying. This way, the eggplant slices hold their shape a little more as they drink up a bit less oil and the result is a heartier, richer dish. Some even flour, egg and breadcrumb their eggplants before frying. And some like to peel the eggplants before frying – it is simply a matter of personal taste and preference. Either way, the most important thing you can do in preparing eggplants for frying is to salt the slices before cooking. Don't skip this part; doing this removes excess water in the eggplants, which means they fry better, improving both taste and texture tenfold. Just don't leave them longer than necessary as they can become too salty.

Pasta con la Ricotta

PASTA WITH RICOTTA

In her wonderful cookbook/memoir *Honey from a Weed* (see page 65), Patience Gray, who lived all over the Mediterranean but finally settled in Puglia, describes exactly what I would do if I had a little basket of made-that-morning, fresh, farmer's sheep's milk ricotta, still dripping with whey: eat half of it fresh for lunch with black pepper and a dish of weeds, then for dinner have it with pasta, tossed with some of the pasta cooking water, parsley, black pepper and nutmeg. When you have the luxury of a very good, fresh farmer's ricotta – which is easy to come across in Italy (less so in other places, I realise) – this seemingly simple pasta dish is something otherworldly.

As you don't need to make a separate sauce – the ricotta itself makes a wonderfully creamy sauce – this is an incredibly quick meal to make. It was, like the *Scamorza alla pizzaiola* (page 43), one of the things that Nonno Mario liked to prepare for himself when coming home late from work, and it is also perfect for serving up to a table full of impatient, hungry mouths.

SERVES 4

320 g (11½ oz) short pasta, such
  as penne, mezzi ziti or sedanini
320 g (11½ oz) very fresh ricotta
1–2 tablespoons extra-virgin olive oil
40 g (1½ oz) parmesan, grated

Cook the pasta in a large pot of salted boiling water (see page 17) according to the instructions on the packet.

Place the ricotta in a mixing bowl large enough to hold all the pasta and add a drizzle of olive oil and the parmesan, and season to taste with some freshly ground black pepper (I find salt is unnecessary because of the parmesan, but taste and adjust to your liking). If you are using any of the additions mentioned in the note (see opposite; my favourite is lemon zest), add them now and stir to combine.

Dip a ladle into the pot of pasta and scoop out about 125 ml (4 fl oz/½ cup) of the cooking water. Add about two-thirds of it to the ricotta

and stir until you have a creamy 'sauce'. If you have a very firm ricotta, you may need a little more of the water.

When the pasta is al dente (with a slight bite to it), drain and immediately toss with the ricotta until evenly coated. Serve immediately, perhaps with some extra ground pepper.

NOTE

If you like, you can add some additional ingredients to the ricotta for extra flavour: the finely grated zest of an organic lemon or orange; any favourite fresh herbs; about 100 g (3½ oz) finely chopped or diced rigatino (or pancetta, guanciale or good-quality bacon), browned separately and drained; a handful of semi-sundried tomatoes (the kind conserved in oil). If you're serving this to children who find the pepper too spicy, try adding some freshly grated nutmeg or a pinch of cinnamon instead – both are common additions to this mild, creamy pasta in Puglia.

53

Ziti al Forno

BAKED ZITI

My mother-in-law Angela's family's version of this southern Italian classic was always a rather simple but satisfying one: tomato sauce flavoured with garlic and basil, layered with cheese (scamorza was always their favourite, but you can also use mozzarella) and, of course, ziti: long, thick tubes of pasta that my daughter likes to pretend are drumsticks – they're very effective when beating on pots. But the way you'll often find it *alla Pugliese* is with the hearty additions of lots of little *polpettine* (hazelnut-sized meatballs), or sometimes even slices of hard-boiled egg, sausage, prosciutto or mortadella. I like to stick to the family's simple version with tomato, basil and scamorza for a weeknight meal, but Marco prefers it with the addition of pork and fennel sausages, crumbled then rolled into small pieces, like quick meatballs.

SERVES 6

80 ml (2½ fl oz/⅓ cup) extra-virgin olive oil
1 garlic clove, thinly sliced
400 g (14 oz) tomato passata (puréed tomatoes)
handful of fresh basil leaves
300 g (10½ oz) ziti
250 g (9 oz) (about 2) pork and fennel
   sausages, skins removed (optional)
250 g (9 oz) scamorza or mozzarella,
   sliced thinly
50 g (1¾ oz) pecorino, grated

Bring a large pot of salted water to the boil (see page 17).

In the meantime, begin preparing a tomato sauce by heating 2 tablespoons of the olive oil in a saucepan over a low, gentle heat. Add the garlic clove and infuse the oil for a couple of minutes, then add the passata and about 250 ml (8½ fl oz/1 cup) water. Season with some salt and pepper and bring the sauce to a steady simmer over a medium heat. Cook for 15–20 minutes, or until the sauce has reduced and thickened slightly. Just before taking off the heat, add about 5–6 basil leaves. Set aside until needed.

Once the pot of water is boiling, add the ziti (they are rather long, so break them in half if necessary to fit them in the pot). Cook until al dente, referring to the packet instructions (minus 1 or 2 minutes of cooking time). Drain and toss the ziti with the sauce until well coated.

Preheat the oven to 180°C (350°F).

To a 20 x 30 cm (8 x 12 in) baking dish, add 1 tablespoon of olive oil and about 2 tablespoons of the tomato sauce. Now add half of the ziti and (if using) scatter over half of the sausage – broken up into small pieces and, if you like, rolled into small meatballs – half of the scamorza and half of the pecorino. Repeat with ziti, sausage and cheese, finishing with the remaining olive oil.

Bake for 15–20 minutes, or until you can see the sauce bubbling around the edges and the top has formed a nice golden crust.

56

THE WAY TO A MAN'S HEART

Pasta with broccoli, a good substitute for cime di rapa, was the first dish I ever cooked for Marco. We didn't know each other very well, were still nervous about what the other person thought and a long way from finding out all the things there were to know about each other. But, so it happened, late one night (much too late to even find a kebab shop open; Marco's usual dinner as a student in Florence at that time), during that cold and miserable February, that I threw together an impromptu meal for a surprised and hungry young man.

I was living alone in the tiniest apartment you could imagine on a winding, steep street near the Ponte Vecchio. It had just one small window but, from that window came the sound of the church bells ringing next door and the view of a single cypress tree. The 'kitchen' was at the end of my bed – it contained a fridge that was actually just a minibar, a sink that could barely fit a pot to wash up and a stovetop with only one working burner.

We were sitting in this makeshift kitchen by my only window. I checked the fridge. It was empty except for one small head of rather leafy broccoli and a piece of pecorino, and I had some garlic hanging around – a fairly dismal offering for the love of your life. 'Do you like broccoli?' I asked, 'I can make you some pasta with broccoli'. 'Perfect,' he replied without faltering. He must have been starving or perhaps he didn't want to disappoint me because I found out later that broccoli was probably the last thing on the planet he would voluntarily choose to eat.

But after I handed him the dish and he took a bite, he looked at me and said, '*Ti sposerò*': I'm going to marry you. And he promptly finished off the whole thing. Two and a half years later we did get married, not too far away from that little apartment.

And, in the meantime, we learned all sorts of things about each other after that pasta dish. I learned that he had never cooked anything in his life (who would, if you had a nonna like his who reigned over the kitchen until her death just two months before?), that his favourite food group was meat (vegetables came in last) and that he had been an impossibly picky eater as a child. But, as an adult, he had become curious and eager to try anything and everything. So, I found other things to cook for him; things that he would marvel at and that would make him happy. Then something else happened – he learned how to cook for me and it's been that way ever since. Almost every day at home, Marco is the one behind the stove, cooking away with an endless curiosity, finding things to make first me, and now our little family, happy.

Orecchiette con Cime di Rapa

FRESH ORECCHIETTE PASTA WITH CIME DI RAPA

Cime di rapa can be literally translated as 'turnip tops', but it's known by many different names – in Florence they're called *rapini*, in Naples *friarelli* and, in Rome *broccoletti*, for starters. This pleasantly bitter, leafy green vegetable with long stems and budding broccoli-like heads, often with tiny yellow flowers, is in the same subspecies as turnips, Chinese cabbage (wombok) and bok choy (pak choy). In English, it is known by even more names, including broccoli rabe (or raab), broccolini (which is actually a different vegetable: the hybrid of regular broccoli and Chinese broccoli or *gai lan*) and *rapini*, like in Tuscany, though more and more (perhaps to avoid all the linguistic confusion), you see it simply referred to as cime di rapa.

They begin to come into season in late autumn and appear in markets until early spring and, depending on when in the season you get them, they may be leafier or have more flowering heads. You use most of the vegetable, the leaves and heads especially, as well as the most tender portion of the long stems. You can replace them with other leafy greens or even with broccoli itself (note that you won't need as much as is required for something leafy; about half), but the beauty of cime di rapa (and the recipes that make the most of it) is its slight bitterness that is tamed and balanced with salt, heat or fat, which is why you often see it paired with anchovies, hot chillies or sausages.

In Puglia, the most well-known way of enjoying cime di rapa is with freshly made orecchiette: pasta shaped like 'little ears'. I learned this orecchiette rolling technique from Maria Grazia, the gracious owner of the stunning Masseria Potenti in Taranto's wine region, Manduria. Orecchiette, like most pasta made in this southern region, is almost always made with *semola rimacinata*, a very fine, pale-yellow semola (durum wheat flour), but sometimes you'll find it made with an interesting flour called *grano arso*, milled from smoked grains so that it has an ash-grey colour similar to buckwheat. I will never forget the first time I ate *orecchiette di grano arso* at Pietro Zito's restaurant Antichi Sapori near Andria in northern Puglia. He paired the smoky pasta with the bright green rambling shoots of the zucchini (courgette) plant and cubes of grilled ricotta salata.

If you don't have the time to make the pasta by hand, you can of course use dried orecchiette, and if you would like to keep this vegetarian, you can leave out the anchovies. However, if you leave them out only because you think you or someone you're serving doesn't like anchovies, I urge you to try it at least once! And then, if you're still certain that you don't like them, pancetta can be used instead. Make sure you get really good-quality anchovies – the kind that are conserved in salt are better than those in oil. The anchovies lend depth, not to mention a delicious saltiness, that together with the bitter cime di rapa are a match made in heaven.

ORECCHIETTE

400 g (14 oz) *semola rimacinata*
   (fine durum wheat flour)
200 ml (7 fl oz) lukewarm water,
   lightly salted

SAUCE

1 kg (2 lb 3 oz) cime di rapa
80 ml (2½ fl oz/⅓ cup) extra-virgin olive oil,
   plus extra for drizzling
2–3 garlic cloves
6–8 anchovy fillets preserved in salt or oil
1 small hot, red chilli, finely chopped (optional)
60 ml (2 fl oz/¼ cup) white wine (or pasta
   cooking water)
finely grated ricotta salata
   (or pecorino or parmesan), to serve

To make the pasta, combine the semola with the water until you have a very soft dough. Let it rest for 30 minutes under a slightly damp tea towel (dish towel) and you'll find it has become even more soft and supple.

Cut the dough into four portions and take one piece, keeping the rest covered with a damp tea towel so it doesn't dry out. Roll the dough into a long snake, no more than 1 cm (½ in) thick, then, with a small knife (preferably something small and simple such as a butter knife with a rounded, slightly flexible tip), cut the snake on the diagonal into pieces about 1.5 cm (½ in), maximum 2 cm (¾ in), long. It is easier to make orecchiette with smaller pieces the first time.

Moving diagonally, use the rounded tip of the knife to roll from one corner to the other. Pick up the piece of dough on the tip of your index finger of your non-dominant hand, then use the second and third finger of your other hand to flip the orecchiette inside out onto the thumb of your non-dominant hand. Continue with the remaining dough until they're finished.

Place the finished orecchiette on clean, dry tea towels to dry out. It's best to let them sit overnight before cooking, or at least for a few hours. If fully dried, they will take 10 minutes to cook; if fresh or partially dried, they will take about 5 minutes.

To make the sauce, bring a large pot of salted water to the boil (see page 17).

In the meantime, prepare the cime di rapa by washing and draining it, then cutting off the thickest stems, keeping all the leaves, heads and the most tender parts of the stems.

Boil the cime di rapa for about 3 minutes (in batches if necessary), or until it is a deep but still bright green and is slightly wilted. Remove the cime di rapa from the water, reserving the cooking water for the pasta.

Rinse the cooked cime di rapa in cold water to halt the cooking process. Squeeze out any excess water, then chop roughly (any flowering broccoli florets can be sliced in half lengthways or in quarters if large) and squeeze again. This can all be done in advance, if needed.

Bring the pot of cooking water to the boil again.

Heat half of the olive oil in a frying pan over a low, gentle heat. Add the garlic cloves and anchovies and, once the garlic begins to get fragrant but not coloured and the anchovies are sizzling and breaking down (about 3–5 minutes), add the chilli (if using), followed by the cooked cime di rapa. Add the wine or pasta cooking water and the rest of the olive oil and continue cooking for a further 5 minutes, or until the greens turn deep green and glossy. Taste and season with salt and pepper, if necessary.

In the meantime, cook the orecchiette until al dente. Drain the pasta, reserving a little of the cooking water, and toss with the cime di rapa until well combined. If you feel it is a little dry, add the rest of the water and an extra drizzle of olive oil. Serve with grated cheese.

61

Ditalini con Cozze e Fagioli

DITALINI PASTA WITH MUSSELS AND BEANS

This is a delicious, hearty and always satisfying combination: plump mussels from Taranto's port and earthy, creamy legumes in a flavourful, fragrant broth, and you can find it in all of Taranto's typical trattorie. The brothy sauce makes this something halfway between a pasta and a soup, and it is always served with a spoon. Instead of borlotti (cranberry) beans, you can also use cannellini beans or even potatoes, peeled, diced into 1 cm (½ in) cubes and boiled together with the pasta.

SERVES 4

1 kg (2 lb 3 oz) live mussels in their shells, beards and any exterior grit removed
240 g (8½ oz) ditalini pasta (or other very small soup pasta)
2 tablespoons extra-virgin olive oil, plus extra for drizzling
1 garlic clove, finely chopped
½ onion, thinly sliced
125 ml (4 fl oz/½ cup) dry white wine
1 large ripe tomato, diced
200 g (7 oz) cooked borlotti (cranberry) beans, drained
1 hot red chilli, finely chopped (optional)
handful of flat-leaf (Italian) parsley leaves, finely chopped

Check over the mussels and discard any that are cracked or open and won't close when gently prodded. Make sure the mussels are cleaned well in fresh water and, if necessary, scrub with steel wool. To open the mussels, heat them in a wide, shallow, dry frying pan over a medium–high heat. Cover, and shake the pan occasionally to help the mussels move around (the ones on the bottom will find it harder to open fully than the ones on top). After about 1–2 minutes, check them and, with a pair of tongs, begin pulling out the mussels that have already opened and transfer these to a large bowl. Continue until all the mussels have opened (any that are still tightly shut can be discarded). Turn off the heat.

Strain the precious mussel liquid left in the pan – either using a very fine-mesh sieve or a regular sieve lined with a paper towel and set over a bowl – and pull out the meat from the shells (reserving some whole mussels to garnish), discarding the shells.

In the meantime, bring a large pot of salted water to the boil (see page 17) and cook the pasta according to the instructions on the packet (minus 1 minute of cooking time).

Heat the olive oil in a wide frying pan over a low heat and gently fry the garlic and onion for about 5 minutes, until the garlic is fragrant and sizzling but not coloured. Pour in the wine and increase the heat to medium. Add the tomato and simmer for a further 5 minutes (if you're using a tomato that you think is probably not as ripe as one that you would find in sun-drenched Puglia, let it cook for 10 minutes, and add a splash of water if you find the liquid is reducing too much).

Add the beans, the mussel meat and their liquid and taste for seasoning (this is important to do only after you add the liquid from the mussels as it can be quite salty). Add the chilli, if using, and some freshly ground black pepper. Bring to a simmer and cook for 2 minutes, then toss over the parsley as you take it off the heat.

Drain the pasta (reserving some of the cooking liquid if you feel you didn't have enough mussel cooking liquid) and serve with the rather soupy sauce (add a splash of the pasta cooking liquid if necessary) of mussels and beans and a drizzle of olive oil. It should be eaten with a spoon.

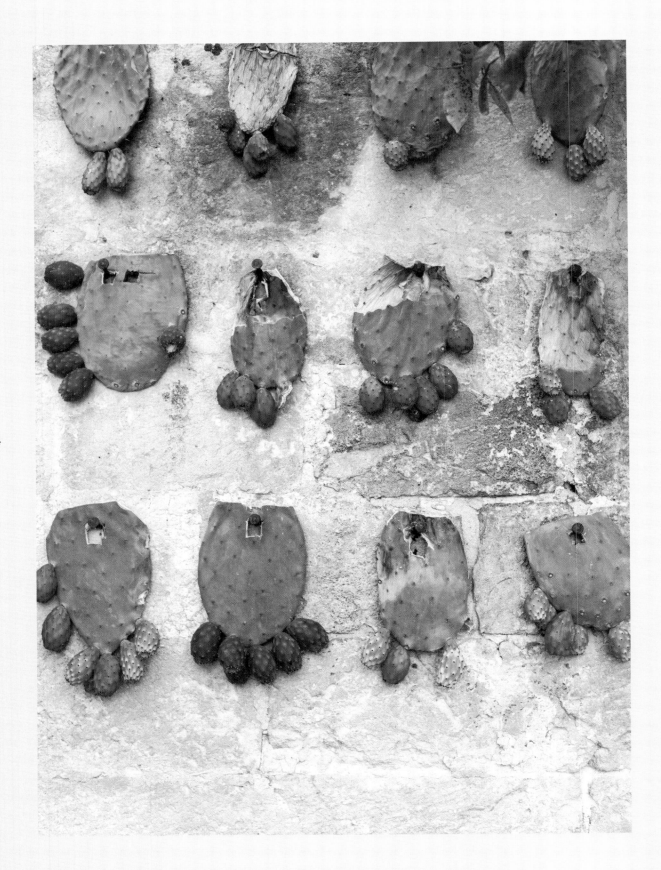

HONEY FROM A WEED

This is one of those few cookbooks I could keep by my bedside, to open at random and become absorbed by a recipe or a story, like the one about sharing a dinner with shepherds on Naxos, the differing opinions of a Milanese and a Salentine diver on what to do with an octopus, or the Catalonian feast that ended with a century old wine that tasted of chocolate syrup. It makes for excellent armchair travelling. Published in 1986, *Honey from a Weed* is part-cookbook, part-memoir. In 1960, English writer Patience Gray met the love of her life, Belgian sculptor Norman Mommens, and they embarked on an odyssey in pursuit of marble for the sculptor's work, which took them to live all over the Mediterranean, from Provence, northern Tuscany, Veneto, Catalonia, the Greek island of Naxos to Puglia. It was in Puglia, in La Spigolizzi – a farmhouse (Gray refers to it as a cowshed) with no electricity – where the couple finally settled in 1970 and where they lived out the rest of their lives. Forever faithful to the place and time and the memories from where she plucked the recipe, Gray's experiences 'living in the wild', as she says, make this a collection of recipes unlike any other; a guide to a way of life that has practically vanished.

Pasta con la Salsa Doppia

PASTA WITH DOUBLE TOMATO SAUCE

It was serendipitous that I read Patience Gray's recipe (which is more of a description of this beautiful summer ritual than actual measurements) for *salsa doppia* while visiting Grottaglie in the province of Taranto, a small, somewhat unglamorous town that has been known for centuries for its artisan ceramic production. Gray describes the oversized, shallow salt-glazed dishes typical of Grottaglie's ceramics – a communal serving bowl where the pasta for the entire family was 'poured, dressed and then dispatched, each member attacking it with a fork'. I had just seen a stack of these ancient dishes in the beautiful ceramic museum-bottega, Casa Vestita, some pieced back together, the large cracks running through them like creases on the palm of your hand. Meanwhile, in Nicola Fasano's ceramic workshop, I found entire dinner sets decorated, like the hand-drawn illustration accompanying Gray's recipe, with a rooster at the bottom of the plate. It is the symbol of Nicola Fasano's ceramics, which Franco Fasano started making in the 60s after discovering a collection of perfectly preserved rooster plates that his grandparents had owned. He, too, recounted that families used to eat from the same large plate – huge, if you were to feed a family of ten like Franco's. The image of the rooster, he said, was to trick you into thinking you might be eating more than what was actually on the plate. The dish may not have had chicken – or any meat – in it, but you could see the drawing on the bottom of the plate and imagine it did.

Although the ancient custom of eating from the same bowl has now disappeared, Gray's *salsa doppia*, which involves layers of home-made, bottled tomato sauce (see pages 176–7), pecorino, orecchiette (home-made if you can – see page 61 – and, if not, your favourite short pasta) and just-picked fresh tomatoes (which in her recipe are quickly cooked, but I prefer to leave them raw), is one worth repeating – I like to do the layering in a pretty bowl to present at the table and then portion out this summery pasta dish into bowls.

SERVES 4

3 ripe tomatoes, diced

1 garlic clove, finely chopped

80–100 ml (2½–3½ fl oz) extra-virgin olive oil

1 small onion, finely sliced

400 g (14 oz) tomato passata (puréed tomatoes)

handful of fresh basil leaves

320 g (11½ oz) short, dried pasta, such as orecchiette or penne

40 g (1½ oz) pecorino, ricotta salata or parmesan, finely grated

Combine the diced tomato, garlic, half of the olive oil and a good pinch of salt in a bowl. Stir well and set it aside to marinate so that the juices are drawn out of the tomatoes.

Bring a large pot of salted water to the boil (see page 17).

Prepare a tomato sauce by gently heating the onion slices in the remaining olive oil with a generous pinch of salt. I like to use a wide pan with curved sides and a bit of depth. Over a low heat, it should take 5–7 minutes for the onions to begin to sizzle and soften without colouring. If the onions begin to brown, add a splash of water or reduce the heat. Add the passata together with about 80 ml (2½ fl oz/⅓ cup) water and a few

whole basil leaves. Season with salt and pepper and simmer over a medium heat for 10 minutes, or until thickened. Set aside.

Add the pasta to the boiling water and cook until al dente, then drain.

In a large, shallow serving bowl, layer half of the pasta, half of the grated cheese and the tomato sugo, followed by the rest of the pasta, the rest of the cheese and the fresh tomato mixture with all its delicious juices. Top with as many fresh basil leaves as you please and present it to the table. When serving at the table, give the whole thing a bit of a stir so that each portion has a bit of everything.

Spaghetti con Ricci di Mare

SPAGHETTI WITH SEA URCHINS

On mine and Marco's first trip together to Puglia, we stayed near a stretch of rocky coastline nicknamed *Ricciolandia*, or 'Sea Urchin Land', as if it were some sort of theme park. Unfortunately, our dreams of eating trays full of freshly opened raw sea urchins right on the rocks were crushed as we had timed our visit all wrong – we were there in June. If only I had known then what all Pugliesi know: that you only eat sea urchins during the months that have an 'r' in them – from May until August they are off the menu, partly out of tradition but also because the sea urchins themselves are practically empty during the summer season when they are in reproduction mode.

Needless to say, we planned our next trip accordingly and enjoyed eating raw sea urchins right out of the shell (the only way to do it in Puglia, with nothing more than a piece of bread to scrape it out with), as well as tossed through pasta for almost every meal. The creamy, orange sea urchin roe is simply tossed through hot spaghetti at the last moment. Many would leave out the tomato, but after tasting a delicious version in a popular family fish restaurant in Taranto called Basile, where fresh tomato was added, I would highly recommend trying it.

SERVES 4

2 ripe tomatoes
1 garlic clove, finely chopped
3 tablespoons extra-virgin olive oil
60 ml (2 fl oz/¼ cup) white wine (or water)
320 g (11½ oz) spaghetti
120 g (4½ oz) fresh sea urchin roe

Score the bottom of the tomatoes with a cross and blanch in boiling water for 30 seconds. Transfer to a bowl of iced water and, once cool enough to handle, peel off the skins and discard. Roughly chop the flesh and set aside.

Bring a large pot of salted water to the boil for the spaghetti (see page 17).

In a wide pan large enough to hold the cooked pasta, heat the garlic in the olive oil over a low–medium heat until fragrant but not browned, about 2 minutes. Add the chopped tomatoes along with a pinch of salt (or to taste). Allow to simmer for 1 minute, then add the wine and simmer for a further 2 minutes.

Add the spaghetti to the pot of boiling water and cook according to the instructions on the packet (minus 1 minute of cooking time), then drain, reserving a glass of the pasta cooking water. Add the spaghetti to the pan and toss with the sea urchin roe, adding a splash of the pasta cooking water if it looks a little dry. Serve immediately.

THE LITTLE SEA

'At midday the water becomes azure blue, and shoals of porpoises glint in the brilliant sun, racing and tumbling, making the spray fly about like diamonds. In the evening the sea seems a mass of molten gold, and the sun sinks fiery red into banks of purple clouds.'

Janet Ross's description of the Mare Piccolo, Taranto's 'little sea', which she noted was teeming with dainty sea horses and sailing paper nautiluses, comes from more than 125 years ago. Ross, an English historian and cookbook writer, lived at the villa Poggio Gherardo (the one Boccaccio supposedly referenced in *The Decameron*), right near my own Florentine neighbourhood of Settignano. Her account of her first trip to Puglia, where her family stayed with Sir James Lacaita near Taranto in 1884, became a book in 1889, *The Land of Manfred, Prince of Tarentum and King of Sicily*. I can't help but compare notes with her.

The sea has long been an important source of industry for Taranto – even as a Greek colony, the city's coins were stamped with molluscs, coral or crustaceans. More specifically, it has been the shellfish that have flourished here. At the time of Pliny the Elder, murex (sea snail) shells from Taranto made a luxurious, highly prized, colour-fast dye known as *porpora* in Italian, or Tyrian purple. During his visit in the late 1700s, the English travel writer Henry Swinburne describes the hill formed from centuries worth of discarded, ancient shells, though by the time novelist George Gissing went looking for it in 1901, he found it had disappeared, 'swallowed up the new Arsenal'.

The Mare Piccolo is home to thirty-four *citri*, freshwater springs, that surge up from the seabed, creating bubbling pools on the sea's surface (Ross notes some are so strong that no boat can go near them). The mixture of fresh and sea water makes the ideal environment for cultivating shellfish such as mussels and oysters, which were introduced to Taranto in the third century BC.

Along Taranto's marina, there is always something going on – someone prying open fresh mussels, fishermen in their rain boots untangling fishing nets, dogs napping, joggers jogging, seagulls chasing fishing boats, divers in wetsuits hauling in buckets full of sea urchins. In the mornings, you can find the fish market, which is nothing more than the fishermen and their impressive offerings on a handful of tables. Live mussels – Taranto's pride, and the main show at the market – strung in enormous, thick garlands are cleaned on the spot by the fishermen, who also remove the shells completely or the half shell. The latter are offered to passersby as proof of their sweet freshness. Even the fish – squid, gobies and small members of the Sparidae family – are so fresh they are all but bouncing out of their shallow styrofoam boxes.

On a Sunday morning, the market is particularly busy, full of locals buying the freshest live shellfish to serve for lunch that day. Oysters are sold whole, for shucking at home. Mussels are sold at five euro per kilogram; prized fresh red prawns (shrimp), so sweet and juicy you only ever eat them raw, just ten euro per kilogram. I watch an elderly woman expertly haggle for a heavy bag of *canastrelle* – tiny, pastel-pink queen scallops – and, curious, I ask the fisherman how they're best prepared. '*Crudi*,' comes the obvious reply – raw. Then he adds, you can also serve them with pasta. But it's pretty clear that when it is live and still squirting water at you, the best way to savour Taranto's seafood is raw, especially the shellfish.

Even the historical accounts of the fish market sound much like what you'll find there today. Henry Swinburne writes of the black mussels that are 'the greatest and most confident supply of the market', which still rings true now. One hundred years later, Janet Ross writes, 'In the little fish-market a conchologist might find amusement for many an hour', noting that there are more than 150 varieties of shellfish found in Taranto's Mare Piccolo. She goes on to describe razor fish, cockles, date mussels, sea urchins, murex (sea snails), pin shells (also known as fan mussels), as well as the familiar long ropes of black mussels, 'All eaten raw'.

Swinburne describes a meal he is offered in a convent in Taranto in 1777, where he is treated 'with the most varied service of shell-fish I ever sat down to. There were no less than fifteen sorts, all extremely fat and savoury, especially a small species of muscle[sic], the shell of which is covered with a velvet shag, and both inside and outside is tinged with the richest violet colour. I tasted of all, and ate plentifully of several sorts, without experiencing the least difficulty in the digestion'.

Fresh seafood is naturally the specialty of every restaurant in both the old and new towns. Some double as fishmongers and have an impressive array of seafood and live shellfish on offer that you can take home. Raw platters of shellfish feature as antipasto on every menu. Depending on the season, you can find yourself in front of a plate of the freshest mussels, both regular and the particularly sweet *cozze pelose* or bearded horse mussels (like Swinburne's velvet-shag covered mussel); oysters; razor clams; sea urchins; *limoni di mare* or the bizarre-looking, rocky 'sea squirts', also known as sea figs; clams of all kinds including warty venus (which have a much better name in Italian: *tartufi di mare*, or sea truffles, to indicate how prized they are) – all to be eaten as is, with perhaps simply a squirt of lemon.

TARANTO

Cozze Ripiene

STUFFED MUSSELS

Taranto's lagoon-like Mare Piccolo (see pages 70–1) is a haven for cultivating mussels, also known as *mitili, muscoli* or *cozze*, which has been the major economic industry in the town for centuries. *Cozze tarantine* come into season from late spring until early autumn. They are small with sweet meat that fills the entire shell and are often eaten raw, opened on the half shell like oysters, with a squeeze of lemon juice, but are also enjoyed baked like the oysters *arraganate* (see page 38), tossed through pasta with fresh tomatoes or beans (see page 62), or stuffed.

This is one of those dishes that requires love and time to prepare – you may want to enlist the help of others with the stuffing part, distribute glasses of wine and enjoy a good chat while you tie each mussel shell. It will be worth it. Otherwise, you can also split this preparation up into stages. A day or two before, you can prepare the sauce and the stuffing. The day before, you can open the mussels and stuff them, then all you have to do fifteen minutes before serving is simmer them in the tomato sauce.

Like *polpette* (see page 84) and many other dishes of Puglia's *cucina povera* tradition, the work that goes into this beautiful meal can cover both a first and second course – the rich tomato sauce, infused with the sea flavour of the mussels, is used to dress pasta for the first course (or even saved for the next day), while the mussels themselves are eaten separately, as the main course. You can, of course, also eat this as one meal – just the mussels, mopped up in their tomato sauce, perhaps with some bread to clean the plate. If you're eating just this, you could generously feed four, but if you are eating this with pasta as well, or other dishes, you could easily serve six. To avoid getting your fingers dirty, you can cut the string before bringing them to the table; the shells just need to be pried back open, which you can do with a knife. Keep a finger dipping bowl nearby for those (like me) who prefer to use their fingers to do this.

74

SERVES 4–6

1 kg (2 lb 3 oz) live mussels in their shells, beards and any exterior grit removed
125 ml (4 fl oz/½ cup) dry white wine
3 tablespoons olive oil
2 garlic cloves
1 x 400 g (14 oz) tin peeled or chopped tomatoes
100 g (3½ oz) day-old or stale country bread, crusts removed
125 ml (4 fl oz/½ cup) milk (approx.)
200 g (7 oz/1½ cups) fresh breadcrumbs (see Note)
100 g (3½ oz) pecorino or parmesan, grated
2 eggs
handful of fresh flat-leaf (Italian) parsley, chopped

Check over the mussels and discard any that are cracked or open and won't close when gently tapped. Rinse well in fresh water and, if necessary, scrub the shells with steel wool.

To open the mussels, heat them in a wide, shallow pan with the wine over a high heat. Cover, and shake the pan occasionally to help the mussels move around (the ones on the bottom will find it harder to open fully than the ones on top). After about 1–2 minutes, check them and, with a pair of tongs, remove the mussels, one by one, as they open and transfer them to a large bowl. Continue until all the mussels have opened (any that are still tightly shut can be discarded). Once completed, filter the precious mussel liquid left in the pan – either use a very fine-mesh sieve or a regular sieve lined with a paper towel and set over a bowl.

In the same large pan, gently infuse the olive oil with one of the garlic cloves (smashed with the side of a large knife) over a low heat. Infuse gently for about 5 minutes, or until fragrant and softened. Add the tomatoes and about 125 ml (4 fl oz/½ cup) water, along with roughly half of the reserved liquid from the mussels. Increase the heat to medium and bring the sauce to a boil. Simmer gently for about 10 minutes, then set aside. Taste for seasoning at this point – I advise you not to add any salt before this moment, or at least not before adding the mussel liquid, as it can be so full-flavoured that you may not need any additional salt, only a touch of pepper.

To prepare the stuffing mixture, soak the stale bread in the milk and finely chop the other garlic clove. Combine the garlic with the fresh breadcrumbs, pecorino, eggs and parsley. Pour over the rest of the mussel liquid and season with pepper. Add the milk-soaked stale bread, squeezed of any excess liquid and crumbled. The consistency should be not too wet, but not crumbly either (if the latter, you can add a bit of the milk the bread was soaking in); it should come together and stay together when you squeeze a spoonful of it in your hand.

Take a spoonful of the filling, squeeze it in your hand to make it compact, then fill an opened mussel shell and wrap a short piece of kitchen string around it tightly to keep it closed. Continue with the rest of the mussels.

Place the stuffed mussels in the pot of tomato sauce and top up with some extra water to ensure the mussels are submerged in the sauce. Cover, and bring to a gentle simmer over a medium heat. Try not to stir the pot too much; if they haven't been tied tightly enough, you risk some of the stuffed mussels opening. Simmer for 15 minutes.

Serve the mussels with a sharp knife to cut the strings (alternatively, cut them all off before serving) and provide finger bowls to clean fingers. If you wish to serve this in two meals, remove the mussels from the sauce and serve the tomato sauce with a long pasta such as spaghetti or bucatini, and the mussels separately as the main course.

NOTE

You'll notice that the so-called 'rule' of no cheese with seafood – that is rigidly applied throughout most of the country – is broken in Puglia. Pecorino and seafood go hand-in-hand in many, if not all, traditional dishes. See Seppie ripiene alla Tarantina *(opposite) for preparing fresh breadcrumbs and substituting with dried breadcrumbs.*

76

Seppie Ripiene alla Tarantina

STUFFED BABY CUTTLEFISH, TARANTO STYLE

This specialty of Taranto home cooking is made with locally fished baby cuttlefish, which are cleverly cleaned whole – to me, they resemble small dinghies holding some delicious cargo. Try to procure completely whole cuttlefish that you will need to clean yourself. If you cannot find these delightfully small cuttlefish, no larger than the size of your palm, you can also prepare this dish with equally small calamari, which can be sliced on one side to create concertina-like cuts where the stuffing will peek through.

SERVES 4

4 baby cuttlefish, approx. 700–800 g
  (1 lb 9 oz–1 lb 12 oz)
80 g (2¾ oz/1 cup) fresh breadcrumbs
  (see Note)
40 g (1½ oz) pecorino or parmesan, grated
1 garlic clove, finely chopped
handful of fresh flat-leaf (Italian) parsley leaves,
  finely chopped
2 eggs
2 teaspoons capers, rinsed and roughly chopped
15–20 green olives, pitted and cut into quarters
3 tablespoons extra-virgin olive oil
125 ml (4 fl oz/½ cup) dry white wine (or water)

To clean the cuttlefish, turn it over so that you have the pale side facing towards you. Run your thumb along the sides, where the wings are attached to the body – you should be able to pierce the skin easily and pull it off along with the wings (which can be discarded or used for something else; they are quite tough). Turn over the cuttlefish and continue removing the skin. You should now clearly see the cuttlefish bone: a large, flat, leaf-shaped piece that lies barely under a second skin. You can pierce this easily with your thumbnail and pull out the bone. Now you should easily be able to see the interior through a very thin membrane. Pierce this with your nail again, or with a sharp knife, being very careful not to break the ink sac, which will look like a little blue bag, or cut through any of the body. You won't need the ink sac for this recipe, but you don't want to pierce it because it makes

an absolute mess and stains everything (but do keep it for tossing through spaghetti with garlic and chilli the next day). Pull out the interior and discard the rest. For the head, cut out the eyes and the hard piece of cartilage that lies behind them without cutting off the head entirely. You should also be able to easily access and pull out the beak, which lies in the middle of the tentacles. Also cut off the two longest tentacles, leaving the rest attached. Rinse well and pat dry with paper towels.

If using whole, uncleaned calamari, pull out the head, which should bring with it all of the entrails, including the quill (you may have to dig a little with your fingers to pry off the bits at the bottom). Pull off the wings that are attached at the bottom of the body and, with this, you should be able to peel off the skin. Rinse the body and ensure it is empty. You can save the wings for another dish (they are a little tough, but are good for a slow braise). The calamari tentacles can be added to the baking dish as they are, or you can chop them finely and add them to the filling.

In a food processor, pulse together the breadcrumbs, cheese, garlic and parsley. Tip the mixture into a bowl and add the eggs, capers, olives and some black pepper (as this is such a flavourful filling, you won't need salt). Divide the filling and stuff each cuttlefish/calamari with this mixture. For the calamari, leave a little room at the top to seal the ends with a toothpick, then, with a sharp knife, make concertina-like incisions about 1 cm (½ in) apart across one side of the body to reveal the filling.

Drizzle the olive oil over the bottom of a baking dish, lay the stuffed cuttlefish over the dish and pour over the wine. Cover with aluminium foil and bake at 180°C (350°F) for 20 minutes, then uncover (save the foil) and continue baking for a further 10–15 minutes. They should be golden on top and a fork should easily pierce the cuttlefish when tender. Remove the dish from the oven, cover with foil again and leave to rest for a further 10 minutes before serving with a spoonful of the pan juices. This is even delicious slightly tepid.

NOTE

It is best to use stale fresh bread as opposed to dried breadcrumbs for moist stuffings, which you can prepare at home by pulling out the bread from a not yet rock-hard loaf of wood-fired bread (a day or two old is ideal), avoiding the crust, especially if it is, like pane pugliese, *a loaf with a strong, hard crust. Tear the bread into small pieces with your hands, then spread it in a layer over a baking tray and leave to dry slightly overnight, covered with a tea towel (dish towel). Alternatively, a faster option is to dry them out in a low oven. Process them in a food processor with some of the ingredients, or bash them with a mortar and pestle to reduce them to crumbs. If you have nothing else, you can also use regular dried breadcrumbs, but use about three-quarters of what is called for and be aware that you may find the filling a little denser and drier than when made with fresh breadcrumbs.*

PANE PUGLIESE

The bread in Puglia is famous all over Italy, in particular *pane di Altamura* from the province of Bari (which has DOP or Protected Designation of Origin status). It is a naturally leavened, enormous crusty loaf with a deep, dark, wood-fired crust harbouring a rich, pillow-soft, pale yellow–hued crumb made from finely-ground semola (durum wheat flour). Its main characteristic is that it is long-lasting, staying soft and delicious for days (even weeks); it has provided sustenance for farmers and shepherds working far from home over the centuries. Ideally, this bread would provide the bulk of the stuffing for this recipe.

Orata al Forno con le Patate

BAKED WHOLE SEA BREAM WITH POTATOES

This classic preparation for whole baked fish is known in the rest of Italy as *orata alla pugliese*. With potatoes on the bottom soaking up all the delicious garlicky, lemony juices, and potatoes on top that get crisp, cheesy and browned, it is one of my absolute favourite ways to prepare a moist, whole baked fish. Use a baking dish that is presentable and you can literally take it from the oven to the table when it is ready (cutting down on washing up). I would serve this with a very simple seasonal salad dressed in extra-virgin olive oil and lemon juice.

SERVES 4

600 g (1 lb 5 oz) potatoes
1 kg (2 lb 3 oz) whole sea bream, cleaned
  and scaled (one large fish or two small
  ones; see Note)
handful of flat-leaf (Italian) parsley leaves,
  finely chopped
2–3 garlic cloves, finely chopped
30 g (1 oz) pecorino or parmesan, finely grated
90 ml (3 fl oz) extra-virgin olive oil
1 lemon, one half cut into slices and the other
  half juiced

Peel and cut the potatoes into very thin slices. Place in a pot of salted, cool water and bring to a simmer over a medium–high heat. Parboil the potatoes for 2–3 minutes, then drain and leave to cool.

Preheat the oven to 180°C (350°F).

Rinse the fish gently and pat dry with paper towel, inside and out. If your fishmonger hasn't done it already, snip the fins of the fish off with sharp kitchen scissors and rub the sides and the cavity with salt and pepper.

Combine the parsley, garlic and pecorino in a small bowl.

Pour half of the olive oil over the bottom of a baking dish large enough to hold the fish. Cover with a layer of potato slices, season with salt and pepper, then scatter over half of the parsley, garlic and pecorino mixture.

Lay the fish on top of the potatoes and slip the lemon slices inside the cavity of the fish. Layer the rest of the potato slices over the top of the fish, slightly overlapping, season with salt and pepper, then scatter over the rest of the parsley, garlic and pecorino mixture and drizzle with the remaining olive oil, followed by the lemon juice.

Cover the baking dish tightly with aluminium foil (to be removed halfway through cooking) and bake until there is a golden crust on the top and the fish is moist and cooked through – a good way to check is to slide a knife along the spine and see if the skin and flesh come away easily from the bone. For larger-sized fish, this should take 35–40 minutes. If using two smaller fish, this should be around 25–30 minutes. Let it rest for 5–10 minutes before serving.

NOTE

Although sea bream is the favourite for this, you can also use whole snapper or sea bass instead. For four people, you can use one whole, large fish weighing about 1 kg (2 lb 3 oz), otherwise choose two small sea bream about 500–600 g (1 lb 2 oz–1 lb 5 oz) each.

THE PRINCESS AND THE POSTMAN

Everyone in the family knows Nonna Anna's story, the one about her being disowned for falling in love with the postman. Marco's uncle, Riccardo Cardellicchio, a journalist, published it in a memoir, *Il Pozzo di Muscioro e altre storie fucecchiesi.* He is the only one who can say he was told this story by elderly Nonna Anna herself, even if he was only a child at the time.

Anna Michela Comasia Maria Calianno was born in Taranto in 1889 into an aristocratic family – Riccardo refers to the Calianno family as *principi* (princes), and therefore to Anna as a princess. She was the paternal grandmother of Riccardo and Angela, my mother-in-law, so is known throughout the family as Nonna Anna. I rummaged through Taranto's archives to try to find out more, first in person, many years ago, when oversized albums of original, handwritten documents (many missing whole pages and with their thick spines duct-taped in place) were pulled down from shelves, and then, thankfully, online once Taranto's council had dutifully scanned all the birth, death and marriage certificates from roughly the 1870s to the turn of the century. I found a treasure trove of information and even though I couldn't confirm the princely title that Riccardo gave them, I could see that Anna came from a very educated, well-to-do family – her father was a physician, her maternal grandfather a surgeon and her mother and grandmother were landowners. They lived in Taranto's main street, Via Duomo – even today, in the crumbling, decaying *borgo* of what is left of the old city, you can see the splendour of the elegant and huge *palazzi* along this artery of the island-city.

One fateful day, a postman delivered something to their door. By chance, young Anna answered. 'He was no Adonis,' Anna recounts to Riccardo in his memoir. He was short and a bit stocky, but she liked him instantly, she said. His name was Nicola Cardellicchio. Raised by a widowed mother, he came from a long line of bricklayers and wool spinners, living in one of the dark and narrow alleys near the port. They could not have come from more different backgrounds.

Anna continued answering the door whenever Nicola passed and their love blossomed, but on discovering Anna's growing interest in the postman, her mother, Girolama, threatened to disown her and she was forbidden to see him again. Anna ran away with nothing but the clothes she was wearing and, arriving at Nicola's doorstep, announced, 'If you want me, here I am'. They married and had nine children in Taranto (Mario was Marco's grandfather), but after the birth of their youngest daughter, and when the First World War had ended, they moved north, to Turin, to look for work, where they stayed until their final days.

Anna was perhaps not an instinctive cook. With her background, it is possible she never learned how to cook. But Angela and Riccardo, her grandchildren, remember her making *polpette* (which became variously known in the family as '*sugo di nonna Anna*' and, oddly, '*amatriciana*'), along with lots of *lesso* (boiled meat), which she made continually. These *polpette* – plump meatballs cooked slowly in tomato sauce, a very traditional dish from Puglia – were taught to her Tuscan daughter-in-law, Lina, who made them so often for her own family that she in turn taught her daughter-in-law, Franca, Riccardo's wife, who continues to make them today for her own grandchildren and great-grandchildren.

Almost everyone makes it exactly the way Anna did, which has a couple of curious steps: she would slice the onion, fry it in a generous dose of olive oil, then, once softened, she would remove it with a slotted spoon. Then she would fry pancetta or rigatino in the same oil and, again, once crisp, remove it. Then this onion and pancetta-infused oil was used for making the sauce. '*Ma non va fatto*,' says Franca, 'You're not supposed to do it,' obviously disapproving of the removal of onion and pancetta from the sauce. Indeed, it seems fiddly, messy and, most of all, wasteful. But Angela, the traditionalist, exclaims, 'But that's the recipe!'

I'm with Franca, who leaves the pancetta in the sauce.

Polpette di Nonna Anna

NONNA ANNA'S MEATBALLS

I've made a few of my own very slight adjustments to the recipe that was recounted to me by both Angela and her sister-in-law, Franca. My main break from the family tradition is to add breadcrumbs. I ate these very similar *polpette* in a lovely little restaurant called Macchiaviva in Grottaglie, in the province of Taranto, and I couldn't help but compare them to Angela's version. The Macchiaviva *polpette*, which were served in a tall, terracotta pot, were so tender that they seemed to melt in the mouth. I asked what the secret was and the chef assured me it was the addition of breadcrumbs to the mixture. In fact, in very traditional recipes for these *polpette*, you will always find breadcrumbs or delicious, spongy, slightly stale, pugliese bread soaked in some milk. Also, if you want to make this with just beef, visit your butcher and choose a cut with quite a bit of fatty marbling (beef ribs, for example, work wonderfully) that they can mince for you.

The best part of this recipe is perhaps the sauce, richly flavoured with pancetta and the *polpette* themselves, which is used to dress pasta (bucatini was Mario's preference) to be eaten as the first course. The rest of the *polpette* are served as the main dish, along with roasted potatoes and a crisp salad. It is, like so many dishes in the Pugliese tradition, a perfect two-course meal.

84

SERVES 6–8

700 g (1 lb 9 oz) minced (ground) beef
300 g (10½ oz) minced (ground) pork
2 eggs
50 g (1¾ oz) parmesan, grated
50 g (1¾ oz/½ cup) dry breadcrumbs
2 tablespoons finely chopped fresh flat-leaf (Italian) parsley, plus extra to serve
1 teaspoon salt, plus extra to taste
60 ml (2 fl oz/¼ cup) extra-virgin olive oil
1 large onion, halved and sliced
80 g (2¾ oz) pancetta or rigatino, finely sliced
700 g (1 lb 9 oz) tomato passata (puréed tomatoes)

Combine the beef, pork, eggs, parmesan, breadcrumbs, parsley, salt and some freshly ground black pepper in a large bowl. Mix very well – using your hands is best – until you have a firm, well-amalgamated mixture. Shape into balls a little larger than golf balls. Set aside on a plate.

Heat the olive oil over a medium–high heat in a deep casserole pot. Sear the polpette in batches, for about 2 minutes each side, until they are lightly browned. (You don't need to cook them through; just colour them.) Once the meatballs are browned, reduce the heat to low and gently fry the onion slices and pancetta for about 7 minutes, or until the onion is softened and the pancetta melts and begins to crisp slightly.

Return the meatballs to the pot. Add the passata, along with 250 ml (8½ fl oz/1 cup) water. Season the sauce with salt and pepper and bring to a simmer over a low–medium heat. Cover and cook for 25 minutes, stirring occasionally. Uncover and cook for a further 15 minutes, or until the sauce has reduced to a rich, thick consistency.

Serve the polpette as is, with plenty of sauce, together with roasted potatoes and a crisp green salad, or set aside the meatballs separately (keeping them warm) and toss your favourite pasta, cooked al dente, through the sauce. Serve this as the first course with some parmesan and parsley, then serve the meatballs as the main.

Peperoni Ripieni

STUFFED YELLOW CAPSICUMS

Nonna Anna taught a few classic dishes from her region to her daughter-in-law, Lina, and this dish became a standard in Lina's repertoire, even when Marco was growing up. It made excellent use of the leftover *lesso* (boiled meat) that Lina prepared daily for her parents. In fact, any time there was a need to use leftover boiled or roasted meat of any kind, or bits and pieces of prosciutto or mortadella (particularly before the early 1960s, when refrigerators became a normal household feature), this dish appeared on the table. Sometimes chopped hard-boiled eggs made it into the mix too. And if it was too difficult to find capsicums (bell peppers) (yellow ones were always favoured in Lina's kitchen, but red are lovely here too), Lina used green tomatoes, eggplants (aubergines), zucchini (courgettes), or a mixture of vegetables all stuffed with this same filling. It is a recipe that changed with the needs of the household. In fact, Lina had the idea that minced (ground) meat was of the poorest quality and refused to use it – if she needed it, she would buy a whole piece of meat and chop it herself, but usually it was leftover cooked meat that was destined for this filling. Although I have listed minced beef for ease, feel free to do the same as Lina – if you find yourself with leftover roast, for example after a holiday feast, this is ideal.

Although in our Tuscan household this is served with the capsicums sitting in a generous pool of sauce and plenty of bread for mopping, in Puglia it is an ingenious dish that serves two courses. The sauce, made sweeter and more delicious from the capsicums, is tossed with orecchiette and grated ricotta salata as the first course, and the stuffed capsicums become the main course. There is also a meatless version, where rice or stale, springy Pugliese bread, crusts off, make up the bulk of the stuffing.

86

SERVES 4

3 tablespoons extra-virgin olive oil

1 large onion, sliced

400 g (14 oz) tomato passata (puréed tomatoes) or tinned chopped tomatoes

500 ml (17 fl oz/2 cups) water or stock (vegetable or beef)

2 medium-sized yellow capsicums (bell peppers)

300 g (10½ oz) minced (ground) beef (or leftover cooked meat of any kind)

60 g (2 oz) mortadella, prosciutto or pork sausage, chopped

1 egg

30 g (1 oz) parmesan, finely grated

30 g (1 oz) scamorza or other good melting cheese, diced

handful of fresh flat-leaf (Italian) parsley leaves, finely chopped

1 teaspoon capers, rinsed and roughly chopped

To prepare the sauce, heat the onion slices in the olive oil with a pinch of salt in a wide pan over a low heat. Cook gently until the onions have softened but not browned, about 10 minutes (if they are starting to brown and you cannot turn down the heat any lower, add a splash of water). Pour in the passata, along with half of the water. Increase the heat to medium and simmer for about 10 minutes.

In the meantime, rinse and slice the capsicums in half lengthways and cut out the seeds (though keep the stem as this helps them hold their shape).

Combine the meat, mortadella, egg, cheeses, parsley and capers in a bowl, season well with salt and freshly ground black pepper and mix well with your hands – Lina liked to add 2 tablespoons of the tomato sauce to the mixture. Divide the mixture into four portions and fill the capsicum halves to the brim and a little more.

Place the capsicums in the sauce along with the rest of the water, cover, and bring to a simmer over a medium heat. Cook for 35 minutes, then uncover and continue cooking for another 10 minutes. This is even better eaten the next day when the flavours have had time to mingle.

Braciole alla Pizzaiola

BEEF SCALOPPINE WITH TOMATO AND MOZZARELLA

Alla pizzaiola is a popular preparation that you can find in various parts of southern Italy, from Naples to Sicily. As you can imagine, the name comes from the use of tomato and cheese, the classic topping for Margherita pizza, and there really are no limits to what you can cook *alla pizzaiola*, from simply the cheese itself (as in the *Scamorza alla pizzaiola* on page 43), to grilled eggplant (aubergine) slices, leftover crumbed and fried meat, even fresh anchovies. But, by far, the most popular dish is the one that brings many Italians a rush of childhood memories: *braciole alla pizzaiola*.

You can use veal or beef (or even chicken) scaloppine for this, which should be sliced ideally no more than about 1 cm (½ in) thick. We like to get a thick sirloin steak that we slice thinly at home. The sauce Marco most remembers from his nonna cooking this for him always had the pungent fragrance of fresh parsley emanating from it, but if your children have a thing against green things floating in their food, leave it off until the end and simply add the herbs for those who like it. Oregano (fresh or dried) is also very typical and we very much like a few capers in there too.

In Puglia, *brasciole* (with an 's') can be found more often in a rolled-up version of *involtini*, where the thin slices of beef are rolled up around a piece of cheese and herbs and held in place with a toothpick before being cooked in tomato sauce. Like so many of these resourceful pugliese recipes, the sauce is used to dress orecchiette or other short pasta, and the meat is eaten as the main course.

88

SERVES 4

4 thin slices sirloin steak, weighing approx.
   120–150 g (4½–5½ oz) each
2 tablespoons extra-virgin olive oil
1 garlic clove, flattened with the side of a knife
400 g (14 oz) tomato passata (puréed tomatoes)
60 ml (2 fl oz/¼ cup) white wine
1 teaspoon capers, rinsed and roughly chopped
   (optional)
250 g (9 oz) fresh mozzarella, sliced
handful of fresh flat-leaf (Italian) parsley
   or oregano, chopped
good-quality crusty bread, to serve

Season the steaks well with salt and pepper on both sides, then set aside.

Prepare the tomato sauce by heating the olive oil in a wide, shallow frying pan over a low heat. Add the garlic clove and leave to infuse the oil gently for a few minutes, but, before it begins to colour, add the passata, followed by the wine and 125 ml (4 fl oz/½ cup) water. Season with salt and pepper. Increase the heat to medium–high and simmer for 10 minutes or so, until the sauce thickens slightly and the smell of alcohol has evaporated. If using the capers, add them to the sauce now.

Place the steaks in the pan, allowing them to be submerged in the sauce. After 2 minutes, flip them over and scatter the mozzarella slices on top. Continue simmering for 2–3 minutes at the most, then turn off the heat, cover the pan with a lid and let it rest for a few minutes (this gives the cheese a chance to melt nicely). Serve, sprinkled with the fresh herbs, with good bread for mopping up the sauce.

Ricotta con Miele di Fichi

RICOTTA WITH FIG HONEY

Fig honey isn't actually honey but a heady syrup made from boiling dried figs. It has the same consistency and golden caramel colour of wild honey. It also has similarities to vincotto, or cooked grape must, which has been used in the south of Italy as a honey and sugar substitute for centuries – both feature in traditional baked goods or are drizzled over fried pastries such as *cartellate* or *pettule*.

Fig honey is easy to make and can be conserved for a long time – even years. Just like honey, you can put this on anything you like, from toast to roasted pork (it makes a great glaze), but the way I like to enjoy this delicious syrup is on good ricotta – the kind that was made fresh that morning and can stand on its own. It reminds Marco of the afternoon snack Nonna Lina often prepared for him: a scoop of fresh ricotta in a small bowl, covered in a sprinkling of sugar. Keep it as an indulgent treat for yourself, or present it with some chopped walnuts or almonds on top as a simple dessert for friends and family.

This makes about 180 ml (6 fl oz) of fig honey, which is more than enough for this recipe, but it's not a bad idea to have extra on hand for drizzling over everything (in fact, you may want to double the recipe). Save any leftovers in a jar and store in the refrigerator or somewhere cool.

SERVES 4

400 g (14 oz/1½ cups) dried figs
400 g (14 oz) fresh farmer's ricotta,
  to serve

Slice the figs in half and place them in a saucepan with 1 litre (34 fl oz/4 cups) water. Let them soak until completely soft and plump. If using dried figs that are particularly dry, you can leave them to soak overnight in the refrigerator.

Place the saucepan over a low heat and let the figs and their water gently simmer for about 1 hour, or until the liquid is reduced by about half. Strain the figs and their liquid in a muslin (cheesecloth)-lined sieve set over a bowl.

When the figs are cool enough to handle, bring the edges of the muslin together and give it a good squeeze and a twist to extract as much liquid as you can. Place the strained liquid back into the pan and bring to the boil (you won't need the fig pulp anymore but don't discard it – it's lovely stirred through thick yoghurt, used in cakes, or as a filling for pastries like the *Bocconotti* on page 91 in place of jam). Reduce the heat and simmer gently for a further 30–40 minutes, or until reduced by another half. It should look like a thick syrup or honey and smell caramelised. Set aside to cool.

To serve, divide the ricotta between four bowls and drizzle a few spoonfuls of fig honey over the top.

Bocconotti

LITTLE CUSTARD AND QUINCE JAM PIES

In the pastry shops around Taranto and the province's white-washed towns such as Martina Franca, you'll find such a dizzying array of *bocconotti* you won't even know where to start. Although they look simple enough from the outside, inside these little pies harbour fillings of custard, custard and sour cherries, sweet ricotta (on its own or studded with candied fruit, pieces of pear or chocolate), apple and cinnamon or jam – all even in the one pastry shop. *Bocconotti* – their name comes from the Italian word for 'mouthful', *boccone*, which is about how quickly you can finish one – from Martina Franca are often made with seasonal jams such as pear, quince or sour cherry, or are filled with custard or both custard and jam – my favourite. And if you're wondering how the *pasticcerie* can tell the difference between one filling and another, each pastry has a special code: some are glazed, some aren't but may have a dusting of icing (confectioners') sugar, others have a little hole or a 'button' of pastry on the top.

This is my personal favourite combination: custard and quince jam. Home-made quince jam makes a really special filling for its pretty pastel colour and unique perfume, but since it can be hard to find fresh quince, apple or pear are good substitutes (and they will only need about half the time to cook and to set). You can, of course, also use a store-bought jam of any flavour you like, but use the best quality one you can find.

MAKES ABOUT 8 PASTRIES

1 egg, beaten (for the egg wash) (optional)
icing (confectioners') sugar, for dusting (optional)

JAM
500 g (1 lb 2 oz) quince, sliced and cored
 but not peeled
juice of 1 lemon
½ vanilla bean, halved lengthways and
 seeds scraped
200 g (7 oz) sugar

CUSTARD
2 egg yolks
60 g (2 oz) sugar
20 g (¾ oz) plain (all-purpose) flour
250 ml (8½ fl oz/1 cup) milk, warmed

PASTRY
250 g (9 oz/12/3 cups) plain (all-purpose) flour,
 plus extra for dusting
100 g (3½ oz) sugar
125 g (4½ oz/½ cup) cold butter, diced
1 whole egg plus 1 egg yolk, beaten (save the
 white for the glaze)
finely grated zest of 1 lemon

For the jam, poach the quince in 750 ml (25½ fl oz/3 cups) simmering water until very soft, about 30 minutes. Drain and pass the fruit through a food mill (mouli). Place the purée back into the pot with the lemon juice and vanilla seeds and bring to a lively simmer. Add the sugar and cook until thick and set, about 30 minutes.

To make the custard, whisk the yolks, sugar and flour until smooth in a small, heavy-based saucepan. Add the warm milk, a little bit at a time, until smooth. Place the pan over a low heat and stir steadily with a whisk until thickened to a consistency like mayonnaise (it will thicken quite suddenly, so pay attention when you see it begin to change). Remove from the heat and pour the custard into a shallow bowl or dish. Cover with some plastic wrap, pressing down on the top of the custard (this is to prevent it from forming a skin), and set aside to cool. Note: if you do not have a heavy-based saucepan or aren't confident about getting a very low heat out of your stovetop, you can use a bain-marie (double boiler) instead. Mix the custard in a heatproof bowl set over a saucepan of simmering water and cook gently instead of directly on the heat.

For the pastry, combine the flour and sugar in a large bowl or in the bowl of a food processor. Add the cold butter pieces to the flour and sugar and, if using your hands, rub the butter into the flour until you get a crumbly mixture and there are no more visible butter pieces. In a food processor, pulse until you have a crumbly texture. Beat the whole egg and the yolk, and add these to the flour mixture along with the lemon zest, then mix until the pastry comes together into a smooth, elastic ball. Let it chill in the fridge, wrapped well in plastic wrap, for at least 30 minutes before using.

When you're ready to assemble the pastries, roll out the dough on a lightly floured surface until it is about 3 mm (⅛ in) thick. Cut out eight discs about 10 cm (4 in) in diameter (see Note). Fill a muffin tray or ramekins with the pastry discs, pressing them down gently so they adhere to the bottom and side perfectly. Prick the base several times with a fork.

Fill the pastries with about 2 heaped tablespoons of custard and 1 heaped tablespoon of jam, or until the pastry cases are almost full.

Gather together the leftover dough and roll it back out to a 3 mm (⅛ in) thickness. Cut out eight discs to cover the tops of the pastries, about 7–8 cm (2¾–3¼ in) in diameter.

Beat the leftover egg white and brush it over the edges of the pastries before putting the discs on top – this works like glue to seal the pastries nicely so the filling doesn't escape. Press down the edges very gently and, if desired, you can also mix up an egg wash with an egg plus 1 tablespoon of water to brush over the tops for a bit of shine. Otherwise, you can leave them plain and dust them with icing sugar once they've baked and cooled.

Bake at 180°C (350°F) for 20 minutes, or until the tops are golden brown and the pastry feels crisp. These keep well for a few days stored in an airtight container in the fridge, if not eaten immediately.

NOTE

For the measurements given in this recipe, I recommend using a standard muffin tin or individual ramekins with a 7–8 cm (2¾–3¼ in) diameter across the top, but, if you already have something slightly different, adjust accordingly. For cutting the discs, you can use cookie cutters or a set of baking rings (which can also be known as cake, tart or mousse rings) in the appropriate sizes. Or you can do what a sensible nonna would: use whatever you have at home. You probably have a glass, mug or small bowl that is just the right diameter. The glass can be pressed right into the dough like a cookie cutter, bowls and mugs with thicker rims can be flipped over and traced into the dough with a small, sharp knife. You can make all parts of this recipe ahead of time; they all keep well for several days in the refrigerator and the pastry itself freezes very well.

CHOCOLATE PUDDING, HOLD THE BLOOD

I once had a boss in Florence who told me, his voice bursting with nostalgia, about a winter festival in his hometown in Puglia where, in an age-old tradition, the town's pigs were butchered and celebrated by the fact that nothing was wasted – right down to the very last drop of blood. The fresh blood was collected in a huge pot and, on the spot, still warm, it was mixed with milk and chocolate and cooked into a dark, decadent pudding. It was the highlight of the festival and the children would line up eagerly for it.

It's a tradition that goes back centuries, particularly in Italy's south; a tradition that recalls times of sheer poverty and makes the most of every available food source, and that is still close to the hearts of those who remember the joy of being able to taste the sweet, slightly metallic zing of this thick chocolate pudding. It is a recipe that is practically extinct as modern tastes and modern butchering practices evolve, helped on by an Italian law made in 1992 banning the sale of pig's blood across many regions. Today, only those who raise their own pigs and have access to fresh blood can still technically make the traditional recipes that call for 'warm' pig's blood (an indicator of just how fresh it should be). More commonly now, the recipe is carried on instead with eggs, flour or cornflour (cornstarch) replacing the blood.

Sanguinaccio al Cioccolato

CHOCOLATE PUDDING

Angela often makes *dolce al cioccolato,* as she calls it, *ad occhio* (by eye) with just cocoa powder, flour, sugar and milk. It's rather like a very thick hot chocolate that she pours over the top of home-made birthday and celebration cakes. She mentioned one day that it was something that her father Mario used to make, usually to adorn his infamous celebration cake (see page 224), and that her mother Lina would make it for afternoon *merenda*, as a snack, sometimes with eggs in it too, like a chocolate custard. It dawned on me that what they were making was really the modern version of *sanguinaccio*: a thick chocolate pudding, minus the blood.

Angela's handwritten notes on Nonna Lina's recipe include flavouring it with vanilla and cinnamon, which are very typical of traditional *sanguinaccio* too. Some other optional flavours to add would be lemon or orange zest, or a splash of rum or your favourite liqueur. I like to add a bit of dark chocolate (the best quality I can find) to Lina's basic recipe, which adds depth and a silky, denser texture to the finished pudding.

This is lovely when eaten completely chilled with a bit of freshly whipped cream and some tart, fresh berries for dessert (making this a really easy dessert to prepare ahead of time as it benefits from an overnight rest in the fridge). But it is equally good when eaten still warm with some simple *biscotti* or savoiardi biscuits for dipping as a decadent afternoon snack on a cold day, the way Nonna Lina would have served it.

SERVES 6–8

150 g (5½ oz) bittersweet (unsweetened)
  cocoa powder
30 g (1 oz) plain (all-purpose) flour
200 g (7 oz) sugar
600 ml (20½ fl oz) milk, warmed
70 g (2½ oz) 70 per cent dark chocolate,
  roughly chopped

Combine the dry ingredients in a heavy-based saucepan. Add the warm milk, a little at a time, so that you create a thick but smooth paste out of the dry ingredients. Continue adding milk, stirring with a wooden spoon or whisk the whole time, until you have a smooth mixture. Place over a very low heat and bring the mixture to a simmer for about 10–15 minutes, stirring constantly. When it thickens enough to heavily coat the spoon (if you drag a spoon across the bottom of the pan, you should be able to see a line momentarily), remove from the heat.

At this point, you have yourself some lovely, thick, decadent hot chocolate, but to continue making puddings, stir through the dark chocolate until melted. Pour the mixture into individual serving bowls or ramekins, or even into one large bowl to serve at the table. Leave it to cool, then put it in the fridge to chill and finish setting completely (if serving with cream and berries, add these on top or on the side at the last moment), or eat it warm as is with biscuits.

Spumone

ICE-CREAM CAKE

A much-loved dessert in southern Italy, *spumone* is a simple dome or loaf-shaped ice-cream cake, served sliced into wedges, which usually reveals two tones of gelato (perhaps hazelnut and chocolate) and a heart of boozy sponge or savoiardi biscuits. Sometimes candied or praline almonds or almond brittle – a treat known as *cupeta* in Puglia – are crushed and mixed through the softened gelato or feature as a layer themselves.

Home-made *spumone* is a treat at any time, and this recipe is a breeze whether made from scratch with the help of an ice-cream machine or with your favourite store-bought gelato. In either case, you just need to start making it a little ahead of time so that you give each component enough time to chill. I've opted for *fior di latte* (milk) and chocolate gelato – family favourites – with an inner layer of savoiardi dipped in coffee (you can use milk for kids or add a splash of rum if it's for adults only) and crushed almond brittle. If making it with store-bought gelato, you'll need to remember to take the gelato out of the freezer to soften slightly before spreading into layers. Feel free to add your own variations – other than the gelato flavours, you may like to use different nuts for the brittle, stir the crushed brittle into the gelato, or use chopped chocolate, candied fruit or anything else that takes your fancy.

SERVES 6–8

50 g (1¾ oz) savoiardi biscuits
60 ml (2 fl oz/¼ cup) espresso coffee
　(or milk), cooled

GELATO

1 litre (34 fl oz/4 cups) full-cream (whole) milk
200 g (7 oz) sugar
100 g (3½ oz) 70 per cent dark chocolate,
　roughly chopped
30 g (1 oz/¼ cup) bittersweet (unsweetened)
　cocoa powder
250 ml (8½ fl oz/1 cup) pouring
　(single/light) cream

CUPETA

100 g (3½ oz/2/3 cup) whole, raw almonds
60 g (2 oz) sugar

For the gelato, place the milk and sugar in a saucepan and heat until it is almost boiling (but watch it carefully; you mustn't let it boil). You should find the sugar has dissolved and the surface of the milk is frothy. Remove from the heat and pour half of the milk into a container.

To the milk left in the saucepan (while it is still hot), add the chocolate and cocoa and whisk until smooth. Let it cool, then chill it in the fridge.

With the container of milk and sugar, leave it to cool completely, then add the cream and chill it in the fridge.

Churn the fior di latte (milk) gelato in an ice-cream machine according to the manufacturer's instructions. You may need to clean and let the ice-cream machine re-freeze in the freezer before doing the chocolate gelato, but check the instructions.

While the gelato is still soft, pour it into a loaf (bar) tin lined with plastic wrap and smooth it out with a spatula. Cover with plastic wrap and place it in the freezer to harden for a few hours or overnight.

Churn the chocolate gelato in the ice-cream machine until soft and creamy.

Meanwhile, make the cupeta. Place the almonds, sugar and 1 tablespoon water in a single layer in the bottom of a frying pan set over a medium heat. Cook until the sugar begins to melt and turn caramel brown. Shake the pan occasionally as the sugar melts, then toss the almonds with the caramel until toasted and well coated. Altogether, this process may only take about 5 minutes. Pour the mixture onto a baking sheet or chopping board lined with baking paper and leave to cool. Before it is completely cool and hardened, chop finely with a heavy knife.

Dip the savoiardi biscuits into the coffee (or milk) and place a layer of them evenly over the fior di latte gelato in the loaf tin. Sprinkle over the chopped cupeta, then smooth over the softened, just-churned chocolate gelato right to the top.

Cover with plastic wrap and freeze until the chocolate gelato has hardened, preferably overnight. Turn out the spumone onto a flat serving plate, remove the plastic wrap and cut thick slices with the help of a large knife dipped in hot water.

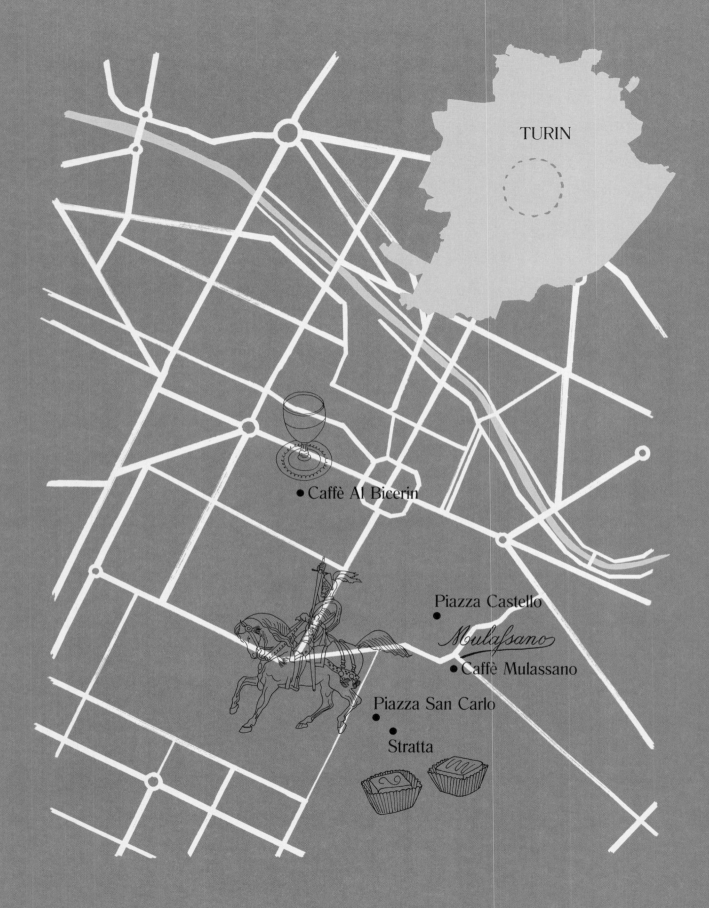

TURIN

• Caffè Al Bicerin

Piazza Castello
•

Mulassano

Caffè Mulassano
•

Piazza San Carlo
•

Stratta
•

Turin

1925

In 1925, Nicola, Anna and their nine children moved from their sun-drenched southern Mediterranean port city to Turin, the elegant, decidedly continental capital of landlocked Piedmont. It was the year their youngest daughter, Iolanda Cardellicchio, was born. Mario would have been eight years old, and although he spent those first eight years in Puglia, as an adult he would always consider himself Torinese, even when he met and married Lina, a dainty young Tuscan girl who had been visiting her cousin in Turin for the summer, and later, during the Second World War, when he moved to Tuscany, where he would live the rest of his life. Lina would often make Mario dishes like *brasato al barolo,* a comforting stew of beef braised in red wine, that reminded him of his home in Turin.

102

This page Lina (on right) with her cousin and sister-in-law, Wanda, who was married to Mario's brother Carlo (in fact, it was while spending the summer with Wanda in Turin that sixteen-year-old Lina met Mario) **Opposite page, clockwise from left** Mario in his military uniform just after leaving Turin; Lina and Mario in the late 1950s in Fucecchio, Tuscany; Lina and Mario holding baby Riccardo in Turin (behind them is Mario's brother Carlo and his family); Lina

TURIN, THE LITTLE PARIS

'Turin is, perhaps, of all the Italian capitals,
the least noticed by travellers, although, in my opinion,
it deserves a distinguished place among them.'

**ANDRÉ VIEUSSEUX,
FOREIGN OFFICER IN THE BRITISH SERVICE, 1818**

Piedmont's capital, Turin (Torino to Italians), is a little jewel of a city, noted, among other things, for its Baroque architecture, cinema, the Fiat factory and for being Italy's first capital and the birthplace of the Risorgimento, which was led by Cavour, a Turin native. It sits along the Po River, with the Alps in the background – a position that led Le Corbusier to call it the city with 'the most beautiful natural location'. It is no surprise that Turin is referred to as the 'Little Paris'; the city's close proximity to France and Switzerland means it naturally feels more continental than Mediterranean. The cobblestone streets, the little iron balconies, grand piazze and royal Savoy palace help paint that picture, but for me one of the main things that contributes to that feeling even more is the active and historical café culture.

Referring to Piazza Castello and Piazza San Carlo, the city's two main squares, Vieusseux noted in 1818 that 'Every day after twelve, one meets the fashionable part of the population, walking up and down, there one finds the best shops, coffee-houses, inns and restaurateurs' – an observation that is still applicable today. Later, Henry James wrote in 1869 (published in *Italian Hours* in 1909), 'To enter Turin then of a lovely August afternoon was to find a city of arcades, of pink and yellow stucco, of innumerable cafés, of blue-legged officers, of ladies draped in the North-Italian mantilla'.

The innumerable cafés are still there and still as elegant as ever, despite (or perhaps thanks to) their age. Caffè al Bicerin has been around since 1763; Stratta, which sits under the arcades of the city's 'salon', Piazza San Carlo, has been known for its exquisite chocolates, sweets and pastries since 1836, while Baratti & Milano has been showering Torino in gold-foiled chocolates from its opulent café in Piazza Castello since 1858.

It's rather hard to ignore the fact that the city claims *gianduja* or *gianduiotti* (luscious, velvety, hazelnut chocolate) and aperitivo (and specifically, vermouth) among its specialties. Being known as the city that invented the aperitivo means the carefully maintained historic cafés serve it up very well. In beautiful spaces, platters of nibbles appear for enjoying with your house-made vermouth (see page 156) on the rocks or mixed in inviting drinks. Coffee is not the rushed affair it is everywhere else in the country; here, when you order a classic *Bicerin* (page 144) you get a tall glass of hot chocolate and coffee smothered in whipped cream that will encourage you to sit and take your time with it. Piedmont is, after all, also the region that is home to the Slow Food Movement.

Grissini Stirati alle Noci

HAND-PULLED WALNUT GRISSINI

Real grissini, hand-made, are far and away a different product from the pre-packed commercial ones you might know and, once you've tried these, you'll understand why Napoleon had an express courier service set up to get freshly made grissini (*les petits bâtons de Turin*) sent to him in France.

Grissini stirati ('pulled' grissini), named for the way they are shaped by pulling from either end of a finger-shaped piece of dough to create long, thin breadsticks, are one of two traditional ways to make artisanal grissini – the other, more ancient tradition is called *grissini rubatà*, which means 'rolled grissini' in Piedmont dialect. These grissini are characterised by a knobbly, rustic appearance, thanks to the hand-rolling method used to make them. Their invention is often dated to the late 1600s – a creation for Turin's young Savoy duke, Vittorio Amedeo II, who found it difficult to digest fresh bread – but some think grissini have been around longer than that. In fact, in the Duomo of Chieri, in the outskirts of Turin, there is a fifteenth-century fresco where you can find a figure chewing on a thin, grissino-like breadstick.

They're the perfect thing to nibble to pass the time as you wait for your main meal, to roll some prosciutto around for aperitivo or even dip into caffè latte for breakfast (as once was the habit). Walnut grissini are one of my personal favourites (they go beautifully with pâté or a cheese platter), but you could also try adding sesame seeds, poppy seeds or any of your favourite herbs in here too – or leave these extra ingredients out entirely for smooth, plain grissini, perhaps just dusted first in some semola (durum wheat flour) before pulling.

MAKES ABOUT 25 GRISSINI

12 g (¼ oz) fresh yeast (or 1¾ teaspoons active dry yeast)
½ tablespoon sugar
250 ml (8½ fl oz/1 cup) lukewarm water, or as needed
2 tablespoons olive oil, plus extra for brushing
500 g (1 lb 2 oz/3⅓ cups) bread flour, plus extra for dusting (see Note)
8 g (¼ oz/1½ teaspoons) salt
100 g (3½ oz) chopped walnuts

In a large bowl, combine the yeast, sugar and water. Let it sit for about 10 minutes, or until the yeast dissolves and becomes foamy. Stir in the olive oil, then add the flour and mix until it comes together into a dough. Knead on a lightly floured surface until smooth, soft and elastic. This should take about 8–10 minutes if doing it by hand (3 minutes if using an electric mixer). Add the salt and walnuts towards the end, kneading until well incorporated.

Flatten the dough into a long rectangle about 1 cm (½ in) thick, then fold into thirds like a book. Place the dough, seam down, on a well-floured or well-oiled surface. Lightly brush the top with extra olive oil, loosely cover with plastic wrap and leave it to rise in a warm corner of the kitchen for about 1 hour, or until doubled in size.

Preheat the oven to 230°C (445°F).

To shape the grissini, take a large, sharp knife and cut the dough across the short side into pieces no more than 1 cm (½ in) wide. Gently pull each piece of dough from both ends, between the thumb and forefinger of both hands. Stretch to the width or length of your baking sheet (don't worry about them being precisely the same length and width; the beauty of these grissini is that they look rustic and hand-made, and that the thicker parts are softer while the thinner parts are crunchier). Place on a lightly oiled baking sheet (or line with baking paper), a few centimetres apart, and bake in batches. Continue with the rest of the dough.

Bake the breadsticks until they are golden, about 10–12 minutes, depending on how thick or thin your breadsticks are. Remove from the oven and cool on wire racks.

Eat them immediately or store them in a paper bag at room temperature for up to 3 days. If they lose their crunch, heat them in a low oven at 150°C (300°F) for about 10 minutes.

NOTE

You could use plain (all-purpose) flour for this recipe instead of bread flour, but the extra protein content in bread flour adds great elasticity to the breadsticks so that when you are shaping (pulling) the dough, you won't risk breaking it. You could potentially pull it longer if you have a large enough tray (and oven) – some grissini are up to 80 cm (2.5 ft) long!

Le Tartine

TARTINES

These tartines were once always the way a dinner gathering, especially for a special occasion, began in my in-laws' household: strictly made with soft white sandwich bread, each one decorated differently from the other following whatever took the cook's fancy. The result reminds me of a bright, decorative plate of nigiri sushi in Tokyo or cicchetti in Venice: something that stimulates the appetite by pleasing the eye with colours and patterns.

Other classic ingredients you could choose from include cooked prawns (shrimp), smoked salmon, cocktail onions, cornichons, cucumber slices, gorgonzola, tinned tuna or grilled (broiled) strips of capsicum (bell pepper) (see page 47). I quite like very thin slices of lemon (rind and all) to pair with the anchovies too. You really are only limited by your imagination.

MAKES 8 TARTINES

30 g (1 oz) softened butter
4 slices soft sandwich bread, cut in half
3–4 slices ham or mortadella
several slices *salame*
3 anchovies preserved in oil or salt, rinsed
2–3 *mozzarelline* (bocconcini or small
    mozzarella balls), sliced
1 hard-boiled egg, sliced
3–4 artichoke hearts preserved in oil,
    halved or quartered
3 cherry tomatoes, cut into slices or halved
3–4 black or green olives, pitted and halved
1 teaspoon capers, rinsed
fresh herbs, such as basil, chives or thyme
mayonnaise, as needed

Butter each rectangle of bread.

Top each tartine with a combination of the ingredients listed, balancing flavours and colours as you please. You can start with a layer of the ham, salame or anchovies. Then top with a layer of mozzarella or egg, then artichoke or tomato and finish with your choice of olives, capers or fresh herbs.

Use the mayonnaise in small blobs as needed (mayonnaise in a tube or piping/icing bag is ideal for this) to keep certain ingredients that can roll about in place: for example the capers, olives or artichokes.

Some suggestions for combinations: ham or mortadella and artichokes; ham and egg; salame and mozzarella; egg, anchovies and capers; mozzarella, olives and tomato.

If not serving immediately, place the tartines on a tray or plate and cover tightly with plastic wrap so the bread does not dry out. Store in the fridge until needed, though keep in mind these are rather good eaten as fresh as possible.

APERITIVO

'Aperitivo' is the word for the ritual of going out for a pre-dinner drink, as well as the sort of drink – an apéritif, to use the French word – and food that you would probably have at such a ritual. It comes from the Latin word meaning 'to open' and, in fact, in Italian you would often describe that mouth-watering sensation you get when you smell garlic sizzling in butter or cake baking in the oven, as something that literally 'opens your stomach'. That's the idea behind aperitivo: a little something to stimulate the appetite so you can fully enjoy your upcoming dinner.

Although it is thought that the idea of a pre-meal drink to stimulate the appetite has been around since Ancient Greek and Roman times, the modern aperitivo ritual is credited to the inventor of the ideal aperitivo beverage – Antonio Benedetto Carpano, who first created vermouth (see page 156) in his bottega in Torino's Piazza Castello in 1786. The habit of taking a glass of vermouth in the evening before dinner became an enormously popular one in a very short amount of time, and soon the bars and cafés of Turin, Milan, Venice, Florence and Rome were serving up aperitivo to enthusiastic, fashionable clients.

Today, aperitivo still plays an important role in Italian social life and is as much about the food and drink as it is about socialising. The classic accompaniments to aperitivi, which are usually bittersweet drinks and cocktails or wine, are small nibbles that can be as simple as bowls of nuts and olives, to more elaborate snacks that head towards antipasto, such as Tartines (page 113) and *Tramezzini* (pages 116–7), for example, but in small portions that won't ruin your appetite.

Tramezzino di Robiola, Sedano e Noci

TURIN-STYLE SANDWICHES WITH CREAM CHEESE, CELERY AND WALNUT

This particular combination is inspired by one you can find at one of my favourite classic Turin cafés, Caffè Mulassano. Other than being the cutest little jewellery-box of a café, this is the place where the *tramezzino* was invented in 1926, according to the little gold plaque near the wooden and glass counter displaying the celebrated little sandwiches. The story goes that newlyweds Angela and Onorino Nebiolo, recently returned to Turin from America where Onorino's relatives had owned restaurants, bought Caffè Mulassano in 1925 and, wanting to serve something new and different, Angela invented the tramezzino – something you now find all over Italy, from every petrol station pit stop to the most elegant of cafés – with its soft, fluffy white bread to serve alongside their aperitivo. It is still what they are famous for today.

SERVES 4–6
AS APERITIVO OR A SNACK

300 g (10½ oz) robiola (see Note)
1 celery stick, thinly sliced
60 g (2 oz) walnuts, chopped
juice of ½ lemon
6 slices soft sandwich bread
   (white or wholemeal)

Combine the robiola, celery, walnuts and lemon juice in a bowl and season to taste with salt and pepper. Spread the mixture onto three slices of the bread and top with the other slices. Cut off the crusts and then cut the sandwiches either into triangles or fingers.

NOTE

Robiola is a creamy, soft-ripened cheese from Piedmont's Langhe region. It's related to stracchino cheese but is butterier, and similar to cream cheese in texture. It can be made with cow's, sheep's or goat's milk, or a mixture of all three, and is wonderfully sweet and creamy, sometimes slightly tangy, depending, they say, on what herbs the animals have been eating. You can substitute with cream cheese or a creamy goat's curd.

116

Tramezzino di Tonno

TURIN-STYLE SANDWICHES WITH TUNA AND SPRING ONION

This is a favourite of Marco's, sometimes with chopped ripe tomatoes in it too. I think it's rather nice to make a mixture of these and the *tramezzini* with robiola, celery and walnuts (see opposite) for aperitivo with friends. Serve with some small bowls of green olives and roasted peanuts or prosciutto-wrapped grissini, along with a glass of house-made vermouth (see page 156) on ice and you have yourself the ideal Turin-style aperitivo.

SERVES 4–6
AS APERITIVO OR A SNACK

200 g (7 oz) tinned tuna, drained
1 spring onion (scallion), finely chopped
juice of ½ lemon
50 g (1¾ oz) mayonnaise
6 slices soft sandwich bread
   (white or wholemeal)

Combine the tuna, onion, lemon juice and mayonnaise in a bowl and season to taste with salt and pepper. Spread the mixture onto three slices of the bread and top with the other slices. Cut off the crusts and then cut the sandwiches either into triangles or fingers.

Bagna Cauda

WARM GARLIC AND ANCHOVY SAUCE WITH CRUNCHY VEGETABLES

In Piedmont, there's a wonderful autumn ritual signalled by the *vendemmia*, the wine harvest; it involves friends getting together around a warm, bubbling terracotta pot (known as a *fujot* in dialect) of *bagna cauda*, a delicious, warm sauce (true to its name), heady with anchovies and mountains of garlic cooked slowly in olive oil. Early autumn vegetables, both raw and cooked, are dipped into the warm sauce, while glasses of *vino nuovo*, young, freshly pressed, local red wine (barbera, nebbiolo, barbaresco and dolcetto) are clinked. The ritual supposedly dates back to the Middle Ages.

Purists will say *bagna cauda* should only be served with capsicums (bell peppers), raw or grilled, then cut into strips, or raw sticks of cardoons, both abundant local vegetables. But it often also accompanies boiled potatoes, slices of whole Baked onions (page 173), raw cabbage leaves, cauliflower, turnips, Jerusalem artichokes or celery sticks.

According to the 'official' recipe, conserved in the Accademia Italiana della Cucina, you need one head of garlic, half a 'glass' of olive oil, 50 g (1¾ oz) anchovies and a piece of butter *per person*. If you're not much of a garlic lover, you might want to consider how nineteenth-century nobles (who had a disdain for the overpowering flavour of garlic) got around this by replacing the garlic with truffles from Alba. Some variations include walnut oil in place of the olive oil, or a mixture of both. And there is a well-known version from Monferrato, which lies to the east of Turin, where the garlic is first cooked slowly in milk, while the anchovies melt into the olive oil, then they are combined into a creamy, mellow sauce.

It's not just a hot dip, though, it's a very versatile condiment and delicious on practically anything. Serve it as a flavourful sauce with roasted meat, dolloped onto squares of polenta (once a traditional peasant's meal) or stirred through some softly scrambled eggs (since nothing is wasted, peasants would reserve the tasty oil left in the *fujot* to fry eggs in – genius). Leftovers are delicious tossed through freshly boiled pasta too.

My favourite way to prepare *bagna cauda* uses significantly less garlic than the 'official' recipe asks for and is inspired by two wonderful old books of traditional Piemontesi recipes: *Piemonte in Bocca* and *Nonna Genia*. The key is low heat and not letting the garlic brown or barely even sizzle.

SERVES 4 AS ANTIPASTO

12 plump garlic cloves
250 ml (8½ fl oz/1 cup) extra-virgin olive oil
100 g (3½ oz) anchovies preserved in oil, drained
50 g (1¾ oz) cold butter

Mince 4–5 of the garlic cloves and finely slice the rest. Combine all the garlic with the olive oil and anchovies in a small saucepan over the lowest possible heat your stovetop has. Cook very gently for about 20 minutes, or until the garlic is soft and fragrant but hasn't browned. Stir occasionally to make sure there is no danger of the garlic browning.

Just before removing from the heat, stir through the cold butter. Serve hot (ideally in a terracotta *fujot*, which keeps the sauce hot with a tea light candle underneath) with your favourite vegetables, raw or cooked, cut into sticks or wedges for easy dipping. If not using immediately, the sauce can be kept in an airtight container in the refrigerator for up to 3 days.

NONNA GENIA

This thoughtful cookbook by Beppe Lodi and Luciano de Giacomi (whose grandmother was Eugenia, the book's namesake) includes, along with stories and theories on this *cucina poplare*, the most traditional recipes from the Langhe area of Piemonte. It is essentially a collection of recipes that grandmothers never wrote down because they knew them by heart. After several trips to the Langhe that left me with many fond food memories (including an unforgettable evening in a trattoria in Grinzane Cavour named after this book), this cookbook was a must-have for me. Published in 1982, it is a book that keeps alive the country recipes of grandmothers that are normally passed on only by keen granddaughters or daughters who have watched and listened and learned – a ritual that is all too quickly disappearing.

Tomini Elettrici

FRESH CURD CHEESE WITH RED SAUCE

Tomino is a classic Piedmont cheese with the fresh version, *tomino fresco*, being a soft, spreadable, curd-like cheese that is usually sold in rolls that can be cut into rounds. Like robiola (see page 116), it is often made with cow's milk, but you can also find *tomini* made with sheep's or goat's milk, or a mixture. It's commonly topped with Salsa verde (pages 126–7) or salsa rossa ('red sauce'), when they're called *tomini verdi* or *tomini rossi*, respectively, and served as antipasto to start off a meal, or for aperitivo with a glass or two of wine. *Tomini elettrici* have an extra element that makes them 'electric' – spicy, hot chilli, pounded into the red sauce, which can vary in consistency depending on if it has been made with tomato sauce, fresh tomatoes or dried tomatoes. They're best when they've been left overnight to marinate – and, like Piedmont's other classic sauces, this is a good one to make a batch of and use on everything from boiled eggs to sandwich fillings and pasta.

SERVES 6
AS PART OF ANTIPASTO OR APERITIVO

300 g tomini or another fresh-curd cheese
   like goat's curd
50 g (1¾ oz/⅓ cup) semi-sundried tomatoes
   (see Note)
2 teaspoons red-wine vinegar
1–2 hot chillies (depending on how 'electric'
   you like it)
1–2 anchovies preserved in salt or oil, rinsed
1–2 tablespoons extra-virgin olive oil,
   or as needed
1 teaspoon capers, rinsed
pinch of fresh or dried oregano

NOTE

Use semi-sundried tomatoes for this, as they are usually still soft and preserved in oil. Proper sundried tomatoes are completely dried and packaged on their own. If using the latter, place them in a bowl, cover with boiling water and let them sit for about 10 minutes, until softened, then weigh them.

If the tomino comes in a log, as in Turin, slice it into six small rounds and set aside on a plate.

Place the rest of the ingredients in a food processor or use a mortar and pestle and pulse or pound until you have a soft, smooth paste. If it looks quite thick, you can add an extra drizzle of olive oil. Top each round of cheese with a spoonful of sauce and, if you have time, let it marinate overnight or for 24 hours before serving.

Any leftover sauce can be stored in a jar in the fridge – but I bet it won't last long.

Vitello Tonnato

ROASTED VEAL IN TUNA SAUCE

A much-loved classic of Piedmont's cuisine – and long a favourite in our household – *vitello tonnato* is often made by roasting a boned leg of veal and serving cold slices with a delicious blended sauce of tuna and home-made mayonnaise. But, in very classic cookbooks such as Ada Boni's 1929 tome, *Il Talismano della Felicità*, and Beppe Lodi's Langhe cookbook, *Nonna Genia* (see page 121), there is a very different way of preparing this dish. In these traditional recipes, the veal is cooked together with the sauce components in a sort of cross-pollination of flavour that enhances both the meat and the sauce. Lodi's recipe does not even include tuna – instead, the veal is marinated in vinegar and water infused with cloves, pepper, cinnamon and bay leaves. The next day, it is cooked in butter with ten anchovies, with boiled eggs helping thicken the sauce. This is somewhere in between.

SERVES 4–8

500 g (1 lb 2 oz) boned veal leg
1 tablespoon extra-virgin olive oil
1 tablespoon butter
1 small onion, sliced
1 teaspoon capers, rinsed
2–3 anchovies preserved in oil, drained
100 g (3½ oz) tinned tuna, drained
125 ml (4 fl oz/½ cup) white wine
juice of ½ lemon, or to taste
1 hard-boiled egg
fresh flat-leaf (Italian) parsley, finely chopped,
    to serve

Remove the veal from the refrigerator 1 hour before cooking.

Preheat the oven to 180°C (350°F).

Season the veal with salt and pepper. Heat the olive oil in a heavy-based ovenproof pan (cast iron is my preference) over a medium–high heat and sear the veal evenly on all sides to a light golden brown. Transfer to a plate.

Add the butter, onion, capers, anchovies and tuna to the same pan and turn the heat down to medium. Cook, stirring occasionally, until the onion is soft, the anchovies have melted and the tuna has taken on a bit of colour, about 7 minutes.

Place the veal back in the pan and pour over the white wine. Cover with a heatproof lid or aluminium foil and place in the oven. Cook for 15 minutes for rare or 25 minutes for medium. Let the veal rest for at least 10–15 minutes before slicing into it. If you are planning on serving this later, leave to cool, wrap well with plastic wrap and refrigerate until ready to serve.

Scrape the rest of the ingredients from the pan into a food processor, along with the lemon juice and the egg, and blend until you have a smooth sauce. Serve this over the top of the veal and scatter over some fresh parsley. This is often served as part of antipasto in Piedmont (when it will easily serve eight), but it also makes a perfect light summer lunch for four with a fresh, crisp salad.

Patate con la Salsa Verde

POTATOES WITH GREEN SAUCE

Salsa verde is one of my favourite sauces of all time. Making it is all about balancing flavours – in particular, the acidity and the saltiness, which for me are what give it so much punch – while the fresh herbs make up the fragrant body of the sauce and the olive oil brings it all together.

Known as *bagnet vert* or 'green sauce' in Piedmont, the combination of ingredients recalls the ancient *vie del sale* – literally 'streets of salt' – that connected the landlocked valleys and hills of Piedmont to the Ligurian sea. Olive oil, salt and anchovies from coastal Liguria made their way through these ancient routes into the heart of Piedmont's cuisine, and they can still be found in some of the region's favourite preparations, like salsa verde and *Bagna cauda* (page 119).

According to Luciano de Giacomi and Beppe Lodi's *Nonna Genia* (see page 121), an indispensable cookbook of traditional recipes from Piedmont's Langhe region, the salsa verde ingredients should be chopped together with a mezzaluna (to give you an idea of just how finely the ingredients need to be chopped, Lodi's instructions say this simple preparation takes an hour), then olive oil and a good pinch of salt are added.

While salsa verde is best known for being the number one condiment for *bollito misto*, which, like Tuscan *lesso* (see page 205) is a traditional dish of boiled mixed meats, there's so much more that this sauce can do. Top rounds of fresh *tomini* (see page 122) with it, blob it onto halved boiled eggs, serve it on Tartines (page 113) or on crostini for antipasto. It's delicious with any roasted meat or grilled (broiled) or steamed fish and – my favourite – tossed through steaming boiled potatoes. This is enough to make about 250 ml (8½ fl oz/1 cup) of sauce because, of course, you'll want more to try on everything.

126

SERVES 4

700 g (1 lb 9 oz) medium-sized potatoes
  (about 6)
3 tablespoons Salsa verde (see below)
2 tablespoons extra-virgin olive oil,
  or as needed

SALSA VERDE

2 anchovies preserved in oil (or 1 preserved
  in salt, rinsed)
2 heaped tablespoons capers
1 garlic clove
100 g (3½ oz) bunch fresh flat-leaf
  (Italian) parsley
about 10 fresh basil leaves
juice of 1 lemon (or 1 tablespoon
  red-wine vinegar)
60 ml (2 fl oz/¼ cup) extra-virgin olive oil

If using anchovies and capers preserved in salt, rinse them under running water to remove excess salt, then place in a bowl of fresh water and leave to soak for 15 minutes. The capers are now ready, but the anchovies need one more step: once soaked, split them lengthways, pulling them apart from the tail. Remove the spine and now you will have two anchovy fillets. If using anchovies preserved in oil or capers in brine, simply drain.

For the salsa verde, blend the anchovies, capers, garlic, herbs and lemon juice together thoroughly using a food processor or hand-held blender. Add the olive oil until you have a paste-like consistency, then season to taste with salt and pepper. This is best prepared at least a few hours before you need to serve it to allow the flavours to mingle.

127

Peel and chop the potatoes into evenly-sized chunks, place in a saucepan and cover with cold water. Add a good pinch of salt to the water and bring to the boil. Cook until the potatoes are tender and can be easily pierced with a fork.

Drain, then, if you want to serve these warm, stir through the salsa verde and olive oil (if you wish, season with extra salt and pepper) while the potatoes are still hot and serve immediately. Or leave the potatoes to cool and stir through the salsa verde and olive oil, then season, toss and serve like a cold potato salad.

Fonduta

CHEESE FONDUE

Piedmont literally means 'at the foot of the mountain' and, indeed, it sits at the bottom of the Alps, bordering both France and Switzerland. So, although many think of fondue as a Swiss national dish, there is a version made in Turin too, which some think is the original fondue. It is less fussy – requiring no wine or liqueur (the Piemontesi save their wine for drinking) and no flour – but, instead, egg yolks, milk-soaked fontina from the Alps and some butter, often laced with grated local white truffles (if you do add this, grate it raw over the fondue right at the table; the heat from the fondue will bring out its aroma).

Like any fondue, however, this needs to be kept warm and it does not keep well (although you can transform any leftovers; see Notes), so make this just before you're ready to serve. Then, all you need is some good bread, sliced into crostini, and to watch it all happily disappear.

128

SERVES 4–6

400 g (14 oz) Fontina cheese, minus the
    rind, diced
400 ml (13½ fl oz) full-cream (whole) milk,
    or enough to cover the cheese
4 egg yolks
40 g (1½ oz) butter
lightly toasted crostini, to serve

Place the diced Fontina in a large bowl and cover with the milk. Let it rest in the fridge for several hours or, better still, overnight.

Prepare a bain-marie (double boiler) by placing a saucepan on top of another slightly larger pot containing simmering water. Place the cheese, milk, egg yolks and butter in the top saucepan of the bain-marie over a medium heat and stir occasionally until the cheese begins to melt, then begin stirring (or whisking if you prefer – I do) continuously until the cheese is entirely melted and you have a smooth, thick and creamy fondue that is neither stringy nor grainy, about 10 minutes (but up to 20 minutes depending on the bain-marie and the cheese itself), ensuring it does not boil.

Serve immediately with plenty of toasted crostini for scooping and dipping.

NOTES

A bain-marie (double boiler) is normally used for making fonduta *– you need a gentle heat so as not to boil the mixture. Ideally, you want to serve the* fonduta *in a* caquelon *(fondue pot), but if you don't have one, use a nice bowl or pot that holds heat well (enamelled cast iron or earthenware, for example). Warm your chosen dish (or dishes, if you would like to prepare individual servings rather than a communal one) in a low oven to ensure the* fonduta *stays warm for longer.*

If you have any leftover fondue, try stirring it through a simple risotto (plain or with diced pear is lovely), or with polenta. It's also excellent smeared on a pizza base in place of tomato sauce – my favourite is with wild mushrooms and paper-thin slices of lardo.

Tajarin al Tartufo

HAND-MADE PASTA WITH TRUFFLES

What differentiates Piedmont's *tajarin* from tagliatelle or tagliolini is the almost exclusive use of yolks in the pasta rather than whole eggs. The famous *tajarin* of retired chef Maria Pagliasso (who is now in her nineties), made with forty yolks for each kilogram (2 lb 3 oz) of flour, became the signature dish of Osteria di Boccondivino in Bra (a town 50 km/31 miles southeast of Turin and the home of the Slow Food Movement) while she was at the helm. Today, thirty years on, her recipe is still on the menu, served with butter and sage, or a classic sugo starring Bra's characteristic mixed beef and pork sausages.

Thanks to the abundant egg yolks, *tajarin* are naturally silky and saffron-hued. Hand-cut to a 2 mm (¹⁄₁₆ in) or, at most, 3 mm (⅛ in) thickness, they are quite delicate and go perfectly with the simple and earthy local sauces – typically, along with the ones mentioned, chicken liver sugo, in broth or with butter and white truffles. This last one hits a soft spot for us, as this part of Piedmont shares something with Tuscany's San Miniato, where Marco was born: both are home to the country's treasured white truffles.

If you can't get white truffles, black truffles can be used the same way here – or go for butter and parmesan (our daughter's preference).

SERVES 4

PASTA
250 g (9 oz/12/3 cups) plain (all-purpose) flour, plus extra for dusting if needed
100 g (3½ oz) egg yolks (about 6)
1 whole egg
semola (durum wheat flour), for dusting

TO SERVE
80 g (2¾ oz) unsalted European-style (cultured) butter
grating of fresh white truffle
grated parmesan, if desired

To make the pasta, sift the flour into a large mixing bowl and make a well in the middle. Tip in the yolks and the whole egg and, with a fork, begin beating the eggs, incorporating the flour around them. Keep working this way until you have a sticky, thick mixture and mixing with a fork is getting difficult. Transfer the sticky dough to a wooden board, along with any flour remaining in the bowl, and, using your hands, begin kneading the dough, incorporating the remaining flour bit by bit. The reason you are doing it bit by bit is because you may not need all the flour, or you may need it all plus more – but, either way, going slowly allows the flour to absorb the liquid better, giving you a better idea of how much or how little flour to use.

Once you have a very firm, smooth (not sticky) dough, cover it in plastic wrap, or place in a bowl covered with a damp tea towel (dish towel) and set aside for 30 minutes.

Once the dough has rested, it should be very smooth and elastic. If you find it has become slightly tacky, dust it very lightly with some flour. Divide the dough into four even pieces and work one piece at a time, keeping the others covered. Pass the dough through a pasta machine, starting with the widest setting and bringing it to the thinnest.

Carefully place the sheet of pasta on a surface barely dusted with flour (wood is best; marble or stone tend to encourage sticking), then cut it into lengths about 30 cm (12 in) long and let them dry slightly while you continue with the next

piece of dough. Letting the dough air-dry slightly (I usually leave it for 5–10 minutes) will help stop the noodles sticking together as you cut the tajarin, however the timing will depend on the humidity in your kitchen and of the dough itself. If it is too humid, the noodles will stick together and won't untangle; if too dry, they will break and crack as you cut them. You can use a bit of flour to very lightly dust the sheets, but be careful not to add too much. Your best bet is to touch the dough and assess how flexible and how smooth, dry or tacky it is and use your best judgement.

Cut the second piece of dough into 30 cm (12 in) lengths and then return to the first batch that has been air-drying. Fold up the dough several times over itself so it is about 5 cm (2 in) long. With a very sharp, heavy knife, cut this piece into thin noodles, somewhere between 1–2 mm (1/16 in), but no more than 3 mm (1/8 in) is ideal. Shake out the noodles to unfold them and dust in some semola. This is where you can tell best if you need to let it dry more or less, as you will see how the dough cuts and whether the noodles stick together or not. Place in a single layer, if

possible, on a tray or board lined with baking paper dusted with semola while you continue working on the rest until all the pasta is cut. You can leave it overnight like this, somewhere cool such as the fridge, to cook the next day, if needed.

Bring a large pot of salted water to the boil (see page 17).

While waiting for the pot to come to the boil, melt the butter in a large, wide pan over a low heat without letting it brown. Turn off the heat and add a grating of white truffle, along with a good pinch of salt to taste.

Cook the pasta for 2 minutes at most. Drain, reserving a small cup of the pasta cooking water, and toss the pasta through the pan of melted butter. If it seems dry, add a splash of the pasta cooking water and toss well so that the sauce becomes emulsified. Transfer the pasta to serving plates and grate over some more white truffle. Serve with parmesan on the side for those who want it – some think it overpowers the delicate scent of the white truffle.

131

Agnolotti al Plin

HAND-MADE PASTA FILLED WITH ROASTED MEAT

This is a dish that you will find throughout Turin's *piole*, the city's classic, old-school trattorie, and it is one of the many preparations that have their origins in the countryside not far out of the city, in the rolling hills and valleys of the winemaking areas of Monferrato and the Langhe.

There are as many versions of *agnolotti* as there are households – and, very often, the ingredients depend simply on what leftovers you have and what you have growing in the garden; a clean-out-the-fridge sort of preparation. In some parts of the Langhe, home-grown rabbit was commonly used as an economical substitute for pork or veal. Sometimes a mixture of all three meats feature, perhaps with a sausage thrown in, some marrow bone or lamb's brains, half a head of cabbage or fistfuls of wild weeds.

As you move across the Piedmont landscape, the shape of *agnolotti* change from small rectangles, similar to regular ravioli, to *plin*, dialect for *pizzicotto* (pinch), which are even smaller and are named for the pinch that encloses the filling in the pasta. You can even find them in half-moon shapes (their name comes from the dialect word *anulòt*, which means ring, for the mould once used to make rounds of pasta to fill). Their special *plin* shape results in little pockets that are perfect for holding the sauce, which is often simply the leftovers found in the bottom of the pan where the meat was roasted, or some melted butter and parmesan.

132

SERVES 4

FILLING

300 g (10½ oz) beef and/or pork,
   cut into large chunks (see introduction)
2 tablespoons olive oil
1 garlic clove
1 sprig rosemary
125 ml (4 fl oz/½ cup) white or red wine
250 ml (8½ fl oz/1 cup) meat or vegetable stock
   (or water)
80 g (2¾ oz/12/3 cups) baby spinach
   (see Note)
80 g (2¾ oz) butter
30 g (1 oz) parmesan, finely grated,
   plus extra to serve
2 egg whites, or as needed (save the yolks
   for the pasta)
freshly grated nutmeg
fresh sage leaves

PASTA

200 g (7 oz/1⅓ cups) plain (all-purpose) flour,
   plus extra for dusting
160 g (5½ oz) egg yolks (about 9; save some
   of the egg whites for the filling and brushing)
semola (durum wheat flour) or extra plain
   (all-purpose) flour, for dusting

To prepare the filling, sprinkle salt and pepper over the meat. Place the olive oil, garlic and rosemary in a casserole pot and heat gently over a low heat to infuse the oil, about 5 minutes. Add the meat chunks, increase the heat to high and lightly brown them on all sides for about 5 minutes. Pour over the wine and, keeping the heat on high, bring it to a rapid simmer and cook for about 10 minutes, or until the wine has reduced significantly. Pour in the stock, lower the heat to low–medium and bring to a simmer. Cook, covered, for 15 minutes, then uncover and continue cooking for a further 15 minutes. The meat should be tender and there should be some delicious pan juices to conserve for the sauce. Set aside, separating the meat from the juices.

In a separate frying pan, wilt the spinach with about 30 g (1 oz) of the butter and a good pinch of salt, about 2 minutes.

To finish the filling, chop the meat into smaller pieces, then place in a food processor along with the spinach and parmesan. Blend until you have a very fine mixture. Add the two egg whites and blend again until you have a soft paste – you can add more egg white as needed to get the right consistency. Add a grating of nutmeg and freshly ground black pepper. Set aside while you make and roll out the pasta.

For the pasta, sift the flour into a large mixing bowl and make a well in the middle. Tip in the yolks (save the egg whites; you will need at least one for brushing the pasta) and, using a fork, begin beating the eggs, incorporating the flour around them. Keep working this way until you have a sticky, thick mixture and mixing with a fork becomes difficult. Transfer the sticky dough to a wooden board, along with any flour remaining in the bowl and, using your hands, begin kneading the dough, incorporating the remaining flour bit by bit. The reason you are doing it bit by bit is because you may not need all the flour or you may need it all plus more – but, either way, going slowly allows the flour to absorb the liquid better, giving you a better idea of how much or how little flour to use.

Once you have a very firm, smooth (not sticky) dough, cover it in plastic wrap, or place in a bowl covered with a damp tea towel (dish towel) and set the dough aside for 30 minutes.

The dough should now be very smooth and elastic. If you find it has become slightly tacky, dust it very lightly with some more flour. Divide the dough into four even pieces and work one piece at a time, keeping the others covered. Pass the dough through a pasta machine, starting with the widest setting and bringing it to the thinnest.

Lay the first sheet of dough on a work surface (wood is best; marble or stone tend to encourage sticking) lightly dusted with flour. Divide in half lengthways so that you have two long pieces, about 6–7 cm (2½–2¾ in) wide. Place half teaspoons of filling (about the size of a hazelnut), no more than 2 cm (¾ in) away from each other,

and about 1.5–2 cm (½ in) from the long edge. Brush some of the leftover egg white along the wider side of the pasta sheet right up against the filling. Fold over the pasta from the edge towards the middle, extending 1–1.5 cm (½ in) past the filling (so you are essentially covering and rolling the filling towards the middle slightly). Pinch the pasta together perpendicular to the work surface between each ball of filling, ensuring there is no trapped air. Trim the long edge of the pasta with a frilled pastry cutter, leaving a 1 cm (½ in) wide flap from the filling. Now, with the frilled pastry cutter, cut decisively between each 'pinch' (it's best to do this from the pinch towards the flap, turning so you are cutting away from you), letting the agnolotti roll over as you cut each piece – this action will help seal the 'pocket' (and, if they don't seal entirely, you can pinch them again individually. You should have little parcels about 3 cm (1¼ in) long by 1.5 cm (½ in) thick.

Place the finished agnolotti on a surface well dusted with semola and continue making them until the pasta is used up.

Bring a large pot of salted water to the boil (see page 17).

In the meantime, heat the reserved pan juices in a wide frying pan along with the rest of the butter and a few sage leaves. Warm until the butter is melted and the sauce is thick – reduce slightly if it is too liquid, or add a splash of the pasta cooking water if it is not loose enough. Taste for seasoning and add salt and pepper if needed.

Boil the agnolotti for about 3 minutes, then drain. Serve them immediately, with a few spoonfuls of the sugo di arrosto (pan juices) drizzled over the top and grated parmesan on the side.

NOTE

Both the filling and the pasta can be prepared the day before you want to make the angolotti. *You can use any meat for the filling. Instead of the spinach, cabbage, any wild weeds or even escarole salad, which has a slightly bitter flavour, are commonly used. Tougher leaves such as cabbage will have to be blanched for a few minutes in boiling water before using.*

Brasato al Barolo

BEEF BRAISED IN RED WINE

This is my idea of a perfect wintry Sunday meal. It's low-maintenance, leaving you free to potter about; but, like other things that are slow-cooked, its main ingredients include time and care. *Brasato* comes from the word 'brasare' (which, interestingly, sounds like 'braise'), or to cook in *brace* or charcoal embers, as stews were once cooked in cast-iron pots set in the middle of the embers of the fireplace and left for hours.

There are just three things you really need to pay attention to for this delicious meal. A whole bottle of Barolo (or any other Nebbiolo-based grape) to cover the meat serves as a tenderiser and flavour-enhancer – I cannot recommend enough that you choose a wine that you like the taste of; it doesn't have to be expensive or even a Barolo, but do pick one that you would happily drink yourself. Don't think that you can use a wine that is corked or tastes like vinegar for this pot roast, as it will, remarkably, still taste like that imperfect wine once cooked.

The beef should have a little marbling or connective tissue in it; if it is too lean it can easily become dry after cooking for so long (some recipes call for lardo or pancetta cut into thin strips to be added to the *brasato* to incorporate some fat and flavour to the otherwise lean, muscular meat of Piedmont's native Fassone cattle). Ask your trusted butcher for a simple roast from around the shoulder. It's known as *sottopaletta* in Piedmont or *cappello del prete*, 'the priest's hat'.

But the best way to ensure a good *brasato* is time. Prepare it well in advance, which makes your Sunday meal even more hands-off. A whole night's rest after cooking it is always a good idea (even obligatory, I would say) – the meat relaxes, the sauce thickens and intensifies – but even a couple more nights will do it good.

137

SERVES 4

- 1.2 kg (2 lb 10 oz) boneless beef in a cut such as chuck roast or pot roast
- 3 tablespoons olive oil
- 1 onion, sliced
- 1 small carrot, roughly chopped
- 1 celery stalk, roughly chopped
- 50 g (1¾ oz) cold butter
- 2 garlic cloves
- 2–3 bay leaves
- handful of mixed fresh herbs, such as rosemary, sage and thyme
- 750 ml (25½ fl oz/3 cups) Barolo or dry red wine
- water or beef stock (see page 205), to cover
- Squashed potatoes, to serve (page 175)
- flat-leaf (Italian) parsley, finely chopped, to serve (optional)

Season the beef with salt and pepper. If necessary, you can tie the beef with kitchen string to help it keep its shape during cooking. Heat the olive oil in a large, heavy-based ovenproof pot if you wish to finish this in the oven (in Italy a terracotta pot is often used). Sear the beef over a high heat for a few minutes on each side until a brown crust develops. Remove the beef and set aside.

Reduce the heat to low. Add the onion, carrot and celery along with a good pinch of salt and half of the butter, and cook gently until the vegetables are soft and translucent, about 10 minutes. Return the beef to the pot, add the garlic cloves and herbs, then pour in the wine. Season with salt and pepper. Increase the heat to medium–high, bring the wine to a boil and let it simmer fiercely for about 5 minutes. Add the water (or beef stock); ideally it should cover the meat or almost cover it. Bring the liquid back to the boil, then cover with a tight-fitting lid and reduce the heat to low. Let it simmer gently for about 2 hours, turning the beef occasionally. Alternatively, if you have an ovenproof pot, you can put this in a moderate oven (set to 160°C/320°F) for the same amount of time.

Remove the meat and set aside. Remove and discard the bay leaves and rosemary or thyme stalks, if you used them. Blend the vegetables and liquid until smooth (an immersion blender is handy for this, otherwise carefully transfer the hot liquid and its contents to a blender, blitz until smooth, then return to the pot). Reduce the sauce over a medium heat, uncovered, until slightly thickened, about 30 minutes. Drop in the rest of the butter and swirl it through the sauce until glossy. Taste for seasoning, adding salt and pepper if necessary.

Cut the beef into slices about 1 cm (½ in) thick and return it to the sauce. You can serve it immediately, though the flavour and texture improve so much overnight, I would always recommend making this the day before. Leave to cool, then store in the refrigerator until the next day (or up to 3 days). Bring back to a rolling simmer, uncovered, for about 10 minutes and serve with the sauce alongside squashed potatoes or soft polenta and sprinkled with chopped parsley.

NOTE

This sauce isn't as thick as a gravy, but if you do prefer a thicker sauce, rather than add flour, you can add more vegetables – up to double the amount. When you blend it, the puréed vegetables will add more body to the sauce. Resting overnight and reheating also gives the sauce a chance to reduce further.

Cioccolato e Pane

GRILLED CHOCOLATE SANDWICH

This is basically a sweet version of the favourite Italian snack known simply as *toast*, which is actually a toasted white bread ham and cheese sandwich. I first had it at Turin's beautiful Caffè Il Bicerin where, sitting on a red velvet bench with Billie Holiday playing in the background, a single flickering candle on the table, and with a glass of their eponymous *Bicerin* (page 144), I have enjoyed the sweetest breakfasts I have ever had. Although it's not quite the same eating this at home, it is, even in its simplicity, so wonderfully decadent. The key is to use Turin's famous *gianduiotto* chocolate, which is a velvety, creamier-than-usual hazelnut chocolate that comes wrapped up like miniature gold bars. Failing that, use the best-quality chocolate you want to treat yourself to.

This is normally made with square sandwich bread – the kind that you would also use for *Tramezzini* (pages 116–7) – which children would probably be overjoyed with. But, if you're making this as a treat with very nice chocolate, I have to say, it's even more delicious with your favourite proper bread. Crusts on or off, it's up to you.

SERVES 1

knob of butter, softened
2 slices bread
50 g (1¾ oz) *gianduiotti* or other favourite,
   good-quality chocolates (about 5), chopped

Butter one side of each slice of bread. Sandwich the chocolate between the unbuttered sides, then toast or grill (broil) on an electric sandwich press or simply in a hot pan with a weight on the sandwich. Toast until the bread is golden and crisp outside, and inside the chocolate is melted – you will need a few minutes on each side.

Bonet

CHOCOLATE AND AMARETTI FLAN

The centuries-old *bonet* is a bit like a Piemontese crème caramel, but flavoured with chocolate and amaretti biscuits. It's a simple, homely dessert that I think needs nothing more than the bittersweet caramel spooned over the top, but it's not always served that way and, if you want to skip the caramel, you could also decorate it with whipped cream, some whole or crushed amaretti, or a sprinkling of finely chopped hazelnuts.

Like other classic Piedmont desserts, such as the Stuffed peaches (see page 148), this is usually made with amaretti di Saronno, the hard and crunchy type, but if you have trouble finding them you can use savoiardi biscuits with a splash of amaretto liqueur. You can also prepare this in a pudding mould or even in individual ovenproof ramekins.

SERVES 6–8

butter, for greasing
175 g (6 oz) sugar
4 eggs
375 ml (12½ fl oz/1½ cups) full-cream (whole) milk, warmed
15 g (½ oz) bittersweet (unsweetened) cocoa powder, sifted
35 g (1¼ oz) amaretti (about 10 small amaretti biscuits), crushed, plus extra for decoration
splash of rum, grappa or similar (optional)

Lightly grease a loaf (bar) tin, approximately 11 x 25 cm (4¼ x 10 in), and preheat the oven to 150°C (300°F).

Place 100 g (3½ oz) of the sugar in a saucepan and shake or tap the pan so that the sugar sits in a flat layer. Add 1 tablespoon water and melt gently over a low–medium heat. Slowly, the sugar will begin to melt and bubble, appearing first to look crystallised. Resist any temptation to stir it, but keep an eye on it until the sugar begins to turn liquid and then a pale amber colour. Now it will begin to change quite quickly. At this point

you can give the pan a swirl to make sure all the sugar crystals melt. As soon as it is completely liquid and the sugar reaches a deep amber colour, remove from the heat and pour it into the greased loaf tin. In total, this should take about 5–7 minutes. Set the pan aside and let it cool.

In a mixing bowl, gently whisk (rather than use an electric mixer, which will result in too many air bubbles) the eggs and the rest of the sugar. Slowly add the warm milk, along with the sifted cocoa powder. Strain the mixture into another bowl, then add the crushed amaretti, and the rum if using. Pour into the tin, over the top of the caramel, then place the tin in a large, deep baking dish. Pour hot water into the baking dish to come halfway up the side of the tin holding the bonet mixture and bake for 50 minutes, or until the top is set and springy.

Remove from the oven and leave to cool completely before chilling in the fridge for a few hours or overnight. To serve, run a thin, sharp knife around the edges of the bonet, then turn it out onto a long, flat plate. Serve in slices with some of the caramel spooned over the top.

143

TURIN

Bicerin

HOT CHOCOLATE WITH COFFEE AND CREAM

Meaning 'little glass' or *biccherino*, this is a decadent drink of thick melted chocolate and espresso with a layer of cream, whipped or barely whipped – my preference is the latter like they do in Caffè al Bicerin, the eighteenth-century bar where it all started. Every historic café in Turin does *bicerin*, but theirs, rightfully so, is exceptional and its recipe is a closely guarded secret. It is served in a wine glass balanced on a saucer, the cold *fior di latte* cream whisked by hand so that it isn't so much whipped as it is thickened to just the right point where you don't need to use a spoon to drink it. As the waitress carefully places the *bicerin* on the little marble table, she gently recommends to enjoy it without stirring – the first gulp is just cool, thick cream, suddenly followed by silky, warm, coffee-spiked chocolate. No wonder Ernest Hemingway said that the *bicerin* should be one of the hundred things in the world to save. This is how I recreate it at home.

SERVES 1

25 g (1 oz) best-quality dark (at least 70%) chocolate, finely chopped
100 ml (3½ fl oz) freshly brewed espresso (double espresso)
2 teaspoons sugar, or to taste
1 teaspoon bittersweet (unsweetened) cocoa powder
80 ml (2½ fl oz/⅓ cup) pouring (single/light) cream

Place the chocolate in a small bowl and pour the hot espresso over it. Stir gently until the chocolate melts.

Combine the sugar and cocoa powder in a small saucepan and add a splash of the coffee and chocolate mixture to make a smooth paste, ensuring there are no lumps. Then add the rest of the coffee mixture and heat gently over a low heat, just until the sugar dissolves and there are no more grains, 1–2 minutes. Do not let it boil. Pour the coffee hot chocolate into a glass.

Place the cream in a jar with a tight-fitting lid and shake (alternatively, you can whisk it by hand in a bowl), until it thickens significantly but still has a pouring (and drinking) consistency. Marco (who used to be a barman during his university days) can do this in less than 10 seconds before it turns into whipped cream, which is not exactly what you want – I take longer, about 30 seconds, to get the cream to the right consistency. Just shake and check as you go, if you don't know your own strength.

Pour the cream into the glass, using a teaspoon to help the cream float in a layer – it will stop the flow of cream just hitting the bottom of the glass. The spoon should be barely touching the hot chocolate and make sure to not let the cream touch the side of the glass.

Zabaione

Pellegrino Artusi has a recipe called 'An egg for a child' in his 1891 cookbook, *Science in the Kitchen and the Art of Eating Well*. It's nothing more than a fluffy, eggy cream, as simple and wholesome a snack as can be, made by whipping the white of an egg and folding it through the egg yolk with sugar. It is rather similar to the more traditional *zabaione* – just leave out the egg white and add a splash of hot espresso (or rum, Marsala or vin santo) instead, which is what the young Marco would get served up by his Nonna Lina for a boost of energy before soccer practice. Lina enjoyed serving coffee to anyone, especially young people! Today, Marco's favourite way of enjoying *zabaione* is with a splash of vin santo, a Tuscan dessert wine.

When using coffee, Nonna Lina wouldn't even use a saucepan, she would just add a boiling hot shot of espresso to the egg and sugar in a teacup and mix until thick, with the heat from the coffee cooking the mixture. Whatever you use, make sure it is good, as nothing is hidden in this simple preparation – and you can, of course, leave out both the alcohol or coffee, taking a cue from Artusi, if you're making this for a child.

PER PERSON

1 very fresh organic free-range egg yolk
2 teaspoons caster (superfine) sugar
50 ml (1¾ fl oz) Marsala, vin santo or other
 young dessert wine (or hot espresso)

Prepare a bain-marie (double boiler) with a few centimetres of simmering water over a low heat (see page 17).

Whisk the yolk and sugar together in a small, heatproof bowl until the mixture becomes pale and creamy. Add the alcohol. Continue whisking with the bowl over a bain-marie, until the mixture is thick, creamy and fluffy. Take it off the heat just when you think it is *almost* ready – like many egg dishes, this is a delicate dish and will continue to cook a little even after you take it off the heat.

Serve warm, alone, with a spoon, or with biscotti, such as the *Paste di meliga* (page 147) for dipping.

145

146

Paste di Meliga

POLENTA BISCUITS

These ancient and deliciously crumbly biscuits (*meliga* meaning *mais*, or corn, in dialect) are often served in Turin's *piole*, the classic trattorie serving traditional dishes. They are offered with a glass of moscato or dolcetto at their simplest, or with a bowl of creamy, freshly whipped *Zabaione* (page 145) at the end of the meal. Cavour, a native Piedmontese, is said to have requested at the end of every meal two *paste di meliga* with a glass of Barolo Chinato, a herby, digestive dessert wine. A real treat.

MAKES APPROX. 22 BISCUITS

100 g (3½ oz/2/3 cup) fine polenta (see Note)
100 g (3½ oz/2/3 cup) plain (all-purpose) flour
75 g (2¾ oz) sugar
125 g (4½ oz/½ cup) butter, chopped
finely grated zest of 1 lemon
1 egg, plus 1 egg yolk

Preheat the oven to 180°C (350°F).

Combine the polenta, flour and sugar in a mixing bowl. Add the chopped butter and process in an electric mixer or, using your hands, rub the butter into the dry ingredients until the mixture resembles breadcrumbs.

Add the lemon zest, egg and yolk and mix until smooth and creamy. The consistency should be thick, but quite wet – enough to put into a piping (icing) bag (even a makeshift one, such as a zip-lock bag). Cut a hole to allow piping the batter in a width of 1 cm (½ in), or use a large enough piping nozzle (this is done with a star-shaped nozzle in Turin's bakeries). Pipe rings about 5–6 cm (2–2½ in) in diameter directly onto a baking sheet lined with baking paper. Bake for 15 minutes, or until the biscuits appear dry on the top and very lightly golden.

If you are not eating them right away, they will store well in a sealed biscuit tin.

NOTE

Look for the finest ground polenta you can get – in Italy you would use a type of polenta called fioretto, *which is most often used for baking (it is pale yellow and as fine as flour), rather than the coarser type used for making cooked, soft polenta.*

Pesche Ripiene

STUFFED PEACHES

This is simply one of the most wonderful summer desserts of all time: nothing more than baked halved peaches stuffed with crushed amaretti biscuits, eggs and sugar. You can find this Piedmont classic in all of Italy's most important historic cookbooks, from Pellegrino Artusi's *Science in the Kitchen and the Art of Eating Well* to Ada Boni's *Talismano della Felicità*.

Artusi calls for a filling of savoiardi biscuits with freshly pounded almond meal (useful to try if you don't have amaretti biscuits). Boni mentions they can be served warm or cold, while De Giacomi and Lodi's Langhe cookbook, *Nonna Genia*, includes cocoa powder and insists they must be served warm or tepid, never cold. I personally love the addition of chocolate to the almond and peach combination, but rather than put it in the filling I like a little dark chocolate grated on top. They are quite delicious with a little *Zabaione* (page 145).

There are two types of amaretti made with essentially the same ingredients of sweet almonds, bitter almonds (which give these little biscuits their name: *amaro* means 'bitter' in Italian), egg whites and sugar. *Amaretti di Saronno*, which come from Lombardy, are hard and crunchy, while *amaretti di Sassello* from Liguria are softer, blonder, almost cake-like biscuits. Both are only just over the Piedmont border, but it's more common to use *Amaretti di Saronno* for this recipe.

148

SERVES 6

7 medium-sized yellow peaches (see Note)
1 tablespoon sugar (optional; see Note)
5 amaretti biscuits, crushed
1 egg yolk
1–2 tablespoons butter, plus extra for greasing
dark chocolate, shaved, to serve (optional)

Preheat the oven to 180°C (350°F).

Rinse and pat dry the peaches. Cut six of the peaches in half, removing the pits and scooping out some extra pulp from each half to make room for the filling. Finely chop this extra pulp and place in a small mixing bowl.

Peel and pit the last peach, then mash or finely chop (depending on how tender the flesh is) the fruit and add it to the bowl, along with the sugar (if using), the amaretti biscuit crumbs and the egg yolk and combine well.

Place the peach halves, face up, in a well-buttered baking dish large enough to fit the twelve halves in a single layer. Fill the peaches with the amaretti mixture and top each with a dot of butter. Bake until the peaches are cooked through, oozing a pretty coloured juice and nicely browned on top, about 40 minutes.

Serve warm or tepid, with some shaved chocolate over the top if you like.

NOTE

Use ripe but not overly mature peaches here; the latter can lose their shape while cooking and become too soft. If using particularly sweet peaches and good-quality amaretti, you may find you can get away with not using sugar in this recipe.

Torcetti

SWEET BREADSTICKS

These are essentially a sweet version of grissini (see pages 109–10): flaky, crumbly breadsticks that are rolled in sugar, twisted into a drop shape and baked until they get sticky, caramelised bottoms. First recorded in dessert cookbooks from the late 1700s, they say *torcetti* were born in the old communal wood-fired ovens of the countryside north of Turin, where they were once made as a special treat to keep children occupied while the adults busied themselves with the bread baking. After the first time I tasted them in Turin, I couldn't walk past a bakery without stopping to get a bag of *torcèt*, as they're known in dialect.

I suggest doing the second rise overnight – pop the dough in the fridge and let the second rise work while you're sleeping. The next morning, the buttery dough – thanks to the chill of the fridge – is also easier to handle. But the best reason for doing this is so that you have warm *torcetti* to dip into your morning coffee without having to wake up too early.

MAKES APPROX. 50 TORCETTI

18 g (½ oz) fresh yeast (or 7 g/¼ oz/
   1 teaspoon active dry yeast)
250 ml (8½ fl oz/1 cup) lukewarm water,
   or as needed
500 g (1 lb 2 oz/6⅔ cups) plain (all-purpose)
   flour, plus extra for dusting
100 g (3½ oz) sugar
170 g (6 oz) unsalted European-style (cultured)
   butter, softened

Place the yeast in a small bowl with about 60 ml (2 fl oz/¼ cup) of the lukewarm water to soften.

Place the flour in a large bowl with 2 tablespoons of the sugar and a pinch of salt. Add the yeast mixture and as much of the remaining water as you need to bring the flour together to a soft, but not sticky, dough. Knead lightly for a few minutes, then place the dough back in the bowl, cover the top of the bowl loosely with plastic wrap or a tea towel (dish towel) and leave to rise in a warm place in the kitchen for 1 hour.

In the meantime, dice the butter and beat with an electric mixer for a few minutes until creamy.

Add the butter to the risen dough and knead or mix until well incorporated. It may be sticky at this point and, if excessively sticky, you can add some extra flour until you have a soft and manageable dough. (If you would like to freeze some or all of the dough, double wrap in plastic wrap and store in a freezer bag for up to 6 months. When ready to use, let the dough come back to room temperature then carry on with the following step.) Place the dough back in the bowl, cover as before and leave to rise for an hour or so in a warm spot, or until doubled in size. You can also leave the bowl of dough in the refrigerator overnight and finish the shaping in the morning (I highly recommended doing this).

If you have done the second rising in a warm spot, give the dough a feel. If it is very soft and sticky, place the dough in the fridge to chill for 30 minutes – this will help harden the butter to make handling easier. If it is still too sticky to work with, add a little more flour.

Place the rest of the sugar on a surface where you can roll pieces of dough, such as a large, flat plate or directly on a clean chopping board, pastry board or kitchen surface.

Preheat the oven to 200°C (400°F).

To begin with, on a very lightly floured surface roll out about half of the dough into a rectangular shape, ideally about 10 cm (4 in) tall and 1 cm

(½ in) thick. With a large, sharp knife, cut the dough into 1 cm (½ in) strips and roll each in the sugar to lightly but evenly coat. Try to stretch the dough out to double the length so you have long 'snakes'. Bring the ends together and pinch into a drop shape. Place on baking sheets lined with baking paper. Continue with the rest of the dough.

Bake in batches, for 12–15 minutes, or until light golden brown. Enjoy warm while you can, but leave to cool completely before storing *torcetti* in a biscuit tin or airtight container.

NOTE

Torcetti *are at their best the day they're baked, but if making this amount seems like too much to get through, you can halve the dough, wrap it very well and freeze it while the rest is going into the fridge for the second rise. Like the grissini, you can keep* torcetti *for a few days and reheat in a low oven to bring back their crunch.*

153

Torta di Nocciole

HAZELNUT CAKE

Italians know that the best hazelnuts in the country come from Piedmont. Even more specifically, they come from the Langhe region, south of Turin: a beautiful and appetising place, seemingly created just for food- and wine-lovers. From gelato to *gianduiotti* chocolates to even, yes, Nutella, hazelnuts are well used in the local cuisine. But my favourite use for them is this humble hazelnut cake, which was once just an autumn and winter specialty: a way to use up excess nuts at the end of the season.

The classic *torta di nocciole* is dense with toasted hazelnuts, giving it a texture that is crumbly and even dry (a good excuse to pair some creamy *Zabaione* – page 145 – with it). Going slightly against tradition, I like to use raw hazelnuts that I pulverise in a food processor just before baking for a moister cake, rather than toasting the nuts or using pre-prepared hazelnut meal. Some like to include a spoonful or two of cocoa powder, but I prefer the nutty flavour of hazelnuts with just a splash of espresso added to the batter.

154

SERVES 8

- 250 g (9 oz) raw, shelled hazelnuts
- 100 g (3½ oz/⅔ cup) plain (all-purpose) flour
- 1½ teaspoons baking powder
- 125 g (4½ oz/½ cup) butter, softened, plus extra for greasing
- 125 g (4½ oz) sugar
- 4 eggs, separated
- 60 ml (2 fl oz/¼ cup) freshly brewed espresso, cooled
- 125 ml (4 fl oz/½ cup) full-cream (whole) milk

Preheat the oven to 180°C (350°F) and grease and line a round spring-form cake tin (approximately 23 cm/9 in in diameter).

Pulverise the hazelnuts in a food processor until fine or like the texture of sand. Place in a large bowl with the flour and baking powder.

Beat the butter and sugar together in another mixing bowl until creamy and pale.

Separate the eggs into two large mixing bowls and whip the whites to stiff peaks. Add the yolks to the butter and sugar and mix. Next, add the dry ingredients, then the cooled espresso and milk, and stir with a spatula or wooden spoon until just combined. Finally, fold in the egg whites.

Gently pour the batter into the prepared tin and bake for 30–35 minutes, or until the top is springy and deep golden brown – a toothpick inserted into the middle of the cake should come out clean. Remove from the oven and leave to cool completely before removing from the tin. This cake keeps well for up to 3 days – store any leftovers in an airtight container or covered in plastic wrap in a cool place.

Vermouth di Torino

MARCO'S TURIN-STYLE VERMOUTH

In the city of aperitivo, vermouth is Turin's quintessential tipple, offered all over the city to be mixed in cocktails or served by itself on the rocks, perhaps with a twist of orange and a maraschino cherry. Created in Turin in 1786, vermouth quickly became a favourite of the city's royalty and has never really gone out of fashion.

Vermouth di Torino is a sweet fortified wine and, if we are going to be precise about it, there are certain things that make a Turin-style vermouth – which has Protected Geographical Indication status – a vermouth. It is composed of three-quarters white wine, which lends the vermouth a pale yellow to amber-red tone (caramelised sugar is permitted as the only colourant, which contributes to the darker colours); it should contain at least thirteen per cent sugar for sweet vermouth, but no more than three per cent for extra-dry or five per cent for dry, and have an alcohol percentage that hovers somewhere between sixteen and twenty-two per cent. It always contains artemisia (wormwood or mugwort): the herb that gives it its most characteristic flavour. But the other aromatics can be composed of your preferred herbs, spices and seeds, and this is what makes one vermouth unique from the next. Aromatics often used in addition to the ones in the recipe below include elderflower, chamomile, marjoram, cloves, mace, vanilla, angelica, sage, thyme, star anise, fennel seeds, ginger, saffron, orange, coriander seed, cardamom and cinnamon.

Some recipes include up to forty different aromatics – like perfume, the more you have, the more unique it is and the harder it is to copy. Marco likes this combination of herbs and spices for this dry vermouth and tends to shy away from sweeter flavours such as vanilla and cinnamon.

MAKES APPROX. 1.2 LITRES (41 FL OZ) VERMOUTH

- 1 litre (34 fl oz/4 cups) trebbiano (or dry white wine)
- 200 ml (7 fl oz) grappa
- 60 g (2 oz) sugar
- 2 g (1/16 oz/1/4 cup) dried wormwood/mugwort leaves (*artemisia vulgaris*)
- 2 g (1 teaspoon) whole aniseed
- 2 g (1 teaspoon) whole fennel seeds
- 10 whole juniper berries
- 1/2 a nutmeg
- pared rind of 1/2 lemon

Combine the wine, grappa and sugar in a bowl and stir until the sugar has dissolved.

Lightly pound the herbs and spices in a mortar and pestle. Add these, plus the lemon rind, to the wine and leave to infuse for 10 days. Do a taste test – if it is too mild, keep infusing for a further 4 days and up to 10. Filter the wine through a fine-mesh sieve or a sieve lined with muslin (cheesecloth) or paper towel, discarding the solids. Bottle and seal the vermouth and store in a cool, dark place for 10 days before serving. Once opened, it should be stored in the refrigerator and used within 2–3 months, as it will oxidise.

Enjoy for aperitivo on the rocks (lots) with a twist of lemon zest squeezed over the top to release the essential oils – Marco's favourite. If you want to turn it into a cocktail, add a splash of vodka.

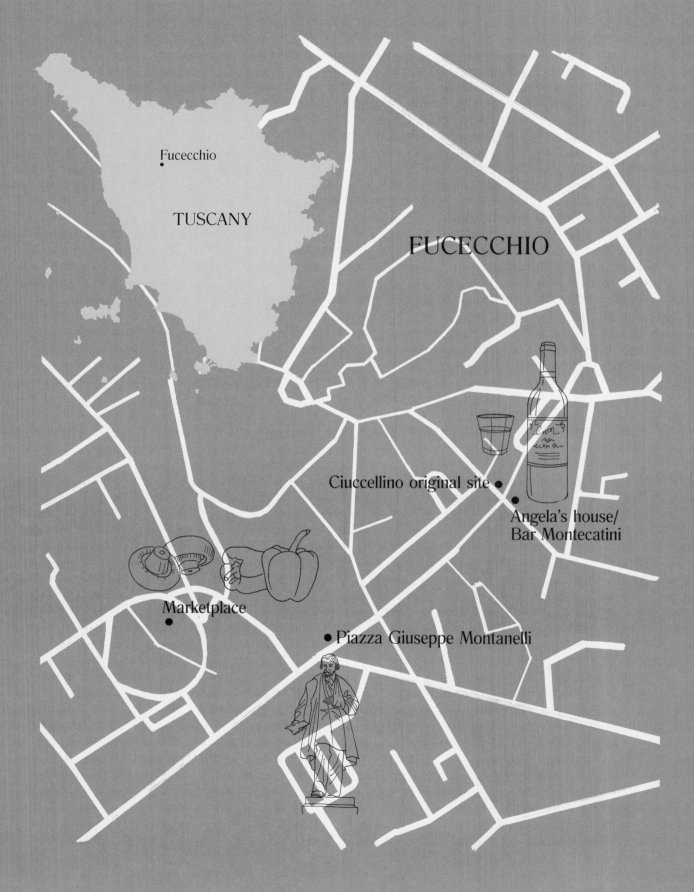

Fucecchio

TUSCANY

FUCECCHIO

Ciuccellino original site ●

● Angela's house/
Bar Montecatini

● Marketplace

● Piazza Giuseppe Montanelli

Tuscany

1945

Lina and Mario had their first baby, Riccardo, on the brink of the Second World War – they moved from Turin to Lina's hometown of Fucecchio, halfway between Florence and Pisa, when Riccardo was young. Then their second child, Angela, my mother-in-law, was born just after the war, in 1946. Post-war Tuscany was a time of simple fare guided by local produce and old traditions. Lina's father, Cesare 'Angiolino' Salvadori, owned a bar in town and her mother, Maria, would prepare all the baked goods for it – her *zuccherini*, a large, ring-shaped, aniseed-studded biscuit, became so well known that they are still considered a specialty of the town today. During reign in her kitchen, Lina loved feeding her family hearty, comforting food, making sure no one went hungry, but she often left the desserts to Mario.

This page Mario, Lina, Riccardo and (in front) Angela
Opposite page, clockwise from left Corso Matteoti, Fucecchio, from Angela's house; Nonno Angiolino and Angela in front of the house; Angiolino's bottega when it was remodelled into a bar in the 1950s (today it's Bar Montecatini)

TUSCANY, FROM SAN MINIATO TO SETTIGNANO

'Tuscany manages to remain so remote, and secretly smiling to itself in its many sleeves. There are so many hills popping up, and they take no notice of one another. There are so many little deep valleys with streams that seem to go their own little way entirely, regardless of river or sea. There are thousands, millions of utterly secluded little nooks, though the land has been under cultivation these thousands of years. But the intensive culture of vine and olive and wheat, by the ceaseless industry of naked human hands and winter-shod feet, and slow-stepping, soft-eyed oxen does not devastate a country, does not denude it, does not lay it bare, does not uncover its nakedness, does not drive away either Pan or his children.'

D.H. LAWRENCE, *SKETCHES OF ETRUSCAN PLACES AND OTHER ITALIAN ESSAYS*, 1932

The hills that D.H. Lawrence gushes about are something that I have always thought give Tuscany its character. That undulating landscape dotted with hilltop towns (we even live in one now, not dissimilar to the hills of Scandicci where Lawrence lived) and the slopes of silvery olive groves and combed vines are still what I think defines the place, though of course not all of it is like that. Renowned twentieth-century journalist Indro Montanelli, who was born in Fucecchio, the town where my in-laws come from, is less flowery in his description: 'The Tuscan countryside is bare, lean, disdainful of trivialities and the superfluous'.

I first read this in the great Anna del Conte's *Classic Food of Northern Italy* (2017), where she uses Montanelli's quote to illustrate how the cooking of this region reflects the character of the people (it is true). Montanelli continues, 'The cooking, too, is lean, made of three or four essentials. And their parsimony is leanness, which should never be confused with meanness, because it is a mental attitude rather than a financial calculation'. Essential, no nonsense, no-frills Tuscan home cooking doesn't have a long list of ingredients or a complicated preparation. I feel as if Montanelli is referring directly to the kind of food that the parents and grandparents of Angela, my mother-in-law, regularly prepared and ate

and that I share here in this chapter – *lesso* (see page 205), the daily boiled beef and its broth, for example, fried artichokes (see page 169), onions roasted whole in their skins (see page 173; does anything more essential exist?) or sturdy, simple baked goods, such as cakes made with lard (see page 240) or the soft, large cookies flavoured with aniseed known in Fucecchio as *Zuccherini* (page 237).

*

Marco was born in San Miniato, an ancient hilltop town that lies strategically equidistant from Florence, Siena, Pisa and Lucca; something that made it an important stop for travellers over the centuries, especially those following the Via Francigena, the ancient pilgrim route between France and Rome. Dominated by a thirteenth-century tower and with practically every well-kept street and palazzo overlooking views of the Arno valley and surrounding countryside, it is an undeniably charming town, only made more appealing by the fact that its hilly oak and chestnut-filled woods are one of the world's rare sources of white truffles, celebrated every autumn in a month-long food festival dedicated to precious *tartufi bianchi* (see page 129).

163

Marco spent his adolescence attending high school in San Miniato and his mother Angela worked for forty years as the school's Latin and Italian teacher, so the town's streets are well-trodden by his family. However, it is in a less picturesque town named Fucecchio – situated at the bottom of San Miniato's hill, and known for its journalists (renowned twentieth-century journalist Indro Montanelli was from here) and leather factories – where Marco's family have lived for generations in the same house that was built by his great-grandfather, Angiolino.

Fucecchio is a rather sleepy town with a crumbling historic centre. There are no restaurants, though you can get excellent artisan gelato and passable takeaway pizza. There are a handful of bars (the kind that serve coffee and pastries), a single-screen cinema, a few Chinese shops (where I go, possibly the only non-Chinese customer, for rice by the scoop, raw peanuts, fresh Chinese vegetables grown in the nearby countryside and condiments that are nearly impossible to find elsewhere) and more hairdressers or barber shops per square metre than any other town I have come across. Every Wednesday morning there is a buzzing market where you can find clothing, fresh produce, plants, fish, cheese, a rotisserie and a van selling just-fried bomboloni and *ciambelle* (or *frati* as they call them in Fucecchio: 'friars' because the round, large doughnuts are reminiscent of the shape of Franciscan haircuts) sparkling with white sugar. They are one of my favourite reasons for visiting Fucecchio on this particular day of the week.

Angela lives in the house where she was born in 1946, on a corner of the main street in town, above the bottega that her grandfather Angiolino once owned. She remembers it from her childhood beautifully adorned with hanging salumi and a stall out the front to entice passersby to visit – it must have worked, as it was always full of people. It was one of the few shops in the lower part of the historic town, and you could buy everything from pasta, bread and baked goods made by her Nonna Maria, to chocolates, salumi, tobacco and salt. It was nicknamed 'Ciuccellino'.

Today it's Bar Montecatini, the sort of bar that opens at six in the morning. It only offers the absolute essentials and has – at all hours – a row of the same old men sitting in plastic chairs out the front, gossiping all day long, their loud voices piercing the house with what Marco calls '*discorsi da bar*', or 'bar chat'. I sometimes wonder whether they even drink coffee there; they seem to only move to follow the sun in the cool weather and the shade in the summer.

We shared the house with Angela for a couple of years, after Marco's father, Carlo, passed away. At one point that house was home to Angela and Carlo, Marco and his sister, Nonna Lina and Nonno Mario and Lina's parents, Angiolino and Maria, as well as Riccardo, Franca and their children. Meals were made to feed many.

Now we have made our home in quaint Settignano, on a Florentine hilltop, surrounded by overgrown olive groves and pointy cypresses, overlooking the rust-coloured terracotta of Florence's rooftops and its Renaissance skyline. Settignano has cooler air and a decidedly slower, village-like pace than the dense centre of Florence below, something that always made it popular among its inhabitants (who included Michelangelo and Mark Twain). There, under a tangle of vines, we rent a small apartment with a tiny kitchen just two metres long. Our kitchen is literally our living room, a fact our eldest daughter complains about, as she would rather not have a sofa in the same room as the oven, but it is probably just as well. The kitchen is always going to be the beating heart of our home.

*

Italy entered the Second World War in the summer of 1940 in the Axis alliance with Germany – only to join the Allies three years later, declaring war on Germany.

Angela's parents, Mario and Lina, moved from Turin to Lina's hometown of Fucecchio in 1943, with their four-year-old son, Riccardo. Mario was in the military and had been sent to nearby Montecatini.

As the war went on, provisions were rationed, staples like milk and flour became scarce and pasta disappeared altogether. Even chestnut flour, which, for so many Tuscans, was the replacement for wheat flour during hard times, became difficult to find. Bread – no longer white, but dark with bran husks – was rationed at 150 grams (5½ ounces) of bread per person. Many local bakers added mashed potatoes to the dough to give it body, since flour was so hard to come by.

Between 1943 and 1944, German soldiers – now Italy's enemies – occupied Fucecchio and hunger was omnipresent. Rice and polenta became the daily meals that replaced pasta and bread. Many poorer families had to walk miles knocking on doors asking for a spare piece of bread, figs were stolen off trees (Fucecchio gets its name from the Latin for 'forest of figs') and what food there was couldn't be paid for. Even at Angiolino's bottega customers' debts were written down in a notebook and added up at the end of the month, a common practice at the time. Knowing full well there was no way for poor families to pay for these debts, Nonna Maria – a generous soul – used to simply cross them out and announce, 'That's paid for!' When she passed away in 1980, people came from all over town, perfect strangers, who had been helped by her and had never forgotten how she saved and fed their families during those difficult times.

In the summer of 1944, the entire family – Angiolino and Maria, along with Lina and little Riccardo – like everyone, were evacuated out of the town centre to the countryside, especially to the padule, the marshlands, to escape the soldiers for forty days. Those who obstinately stayed in the city put themselves in danger – Angiolino's sister Giulia and her husband came back to town and were killed trying to stop some soldiers from raping a young woman. But, five days later, on the twenty-third of August, a week and a half before the Allies reached Fucecchio to liberate it, German soldiers marched out to the swamps and murdered 174 men, women and children – civilians from many of the nearby town centres, from newborns to the elderly.

When the Allies came through Fucecchio, the Germans fled and the townspeople returned from the countryside. Angiolino and his family returned to their house and found it destroyed and everything in it stolen by German soldiers and Italian fascists who knew of Angiolino's anti-fascist stance. They didn't even have a

fork to eat with, as Lina used to tell Angela. For years, Lina would find her tablecloths and sheets hanging out of windows among the laundry of others in town – presumably the thieves.

Two years later, Angela, my mother-in-law, was born and Mario and Lina were settled in Angiolino's house in Fucecchio. By the end of the 1940s, things had returned to normal. Food was cheap and plentiful. The *alimentari* shelves were re-stocked and, in 1952, the family house was finally rebuilt, as was the bottega, which became the bar that sits under the house now, with a large piece of land out the back for customers who came from near and far to play *bocce* (boules) under an enormous fig tree.

Pinzimonio

RAW VEGETABLES FOR ANTIPASTO

Nonna Lina would prepare this classic Tuscan antipasto of raw vegetables in a *coppa*, a glass bowl with legs, with extra-virgin olive oil simply seasoned with salt and pepper for dipping. I always look forward to starting a Tuscan meal with fresh, crunchy vegetables dipped in peppery olive oil; they are so easy to prepare and are such a refreshing contrast to the rest of the (relatively heavy) Tuscan meal.

The following 'recipe' is mostly a suggestion and reflects what you would typically find at any time in our house and probably most Tuscan trattorie or homes that still do *pinzimonio*. Let the season guide you – cucumber and cherry tomatoes in summer and radicchio or endive sliced lengthways in winter are also favourite additions of ours. Use your best olive oil for this.

SERVES 4

2 carrots
2 celery stalks
1 fennel bulb
bunch of radishes
extra-virgin olive oil

166

Peel and cut the carrot into sticks. Rinse and pat dry the celery, then cut into sticks the same size as the carrot. Peel off the outer layer of the fennel bulb and trim off the hard root end on the bottom and the fronds on the top (I like to save these for salads). Cut the fennel in half lengthways, then place the two pieces, flat-side down, and cut lengthways into 3–5 mm (¼ in) slices.

Rinse the radishes and pull off their leaves. Trim any roots and halve them if they are large, but keep small ones whole.

If preparing well in advance, keep the carrot and celery sticks covered with fresh water in a bowl in the fridge until needed – the cold water will keep them very crunchy. Prepare the fennel at the last minute so it doesn't oxidise, or place it in a separate bowl of fresh water with the juice of a lemon until needed. The vegetables will keep this way for several hours or overnight. Drain and pat dry before serving.

Pour olive oil into a small bowl and add a pinch of salt and freshly ground black pepper. Stir and serve with the cut vegetables, which are to be dipped in the olive oil.

Frittata di Patate

POTATO FRITTATA

A satisfying, filling meal that is good cold for picnics, maybe sandwiched between *schiacciata* as a panino (like they do at our favourite local spot, Caffè Desiderio) or just out of the pan with a salad for a light lunch or dinner. The frittata is a great way of making a meal out of seemingly nothing. Just try to resist overfilling it or making it too heavy and stick to this formula: pick a seasonal vegetable, cook it until tender in a large pan, then crack one egg per person into it and add cheese. It should just be enough egg to hold the vegetables together. Nonna Lina would make this with finely sliced potatoes and lots of parmesan. I like it with a good melting cheese like provolone or asiago. Depending on the season, you can substitute thinly sliced artichokes (with mint instead of rosemary), fennel (with their green tops) or green tomatoes (with basil).

SERVES 4

400 g (14 oz) potatoes (about 2 medium–large)
3 tablespoons extra-virgin olive oil
1 fresh rosemary sprig, leaves picked and
    finely chopped
4 eggs, beaten until just combined
50 g (1¾ oz) parmesan or provolone,
    grated or finely sliced

Peel then slice the potatoes as thin as you can (if needed, first slice the potatoes in half lengthways). Place them in an ovenproof frying pan with the olive oil and rosemary over a medium heat. Add about 60 ml (2 fl oz/¼ cup) water, cover the pan and stir every now and then to evenly distribute and brown the potatoes (add more water as needed). You can boil them if you prefer, but I like cooking them directly in the pan as it gives them an opportunity to get browned edges and the stirring breaks them up a little, giving you creamy bits. Depending on the quality, type and age of the potatoes, it will take about 25–30 minutes until they are tender and cooked through (check with a fork).

Preheat the oven to 180°C (350°F).

Pour the beaten eggs over the top of the potatoes, tipping the pan to ensure that the eggs cover the whole thing. Sprinkle over the cheese and continue cooking on the stovetop for a further 5 minutes, covered. Transfer the pan to the oven to finish cooking the top until the cheese is melted and the egg is set, about 5 minutes.

NOTE

Use the best frying pan you have for cooking eggs in. In other words, something non-stick and heatproof. Personally, I love a well-seasoned cast-iron pan for frittata as it can also go directly from stovetop to oven.

Carciofi Fritti

DEEP-FRIED BATTERED ARTICHOKES

These are to be eaten all winter and spring, piping hot, and with crumbed lamb chops (see page 202) at Easter. Some Tuscans like only to dust the artichokes in flour before deep-frying but, in our house, we're all in agreement that there's nothing better than a battered, wine-spiked, deep-fried artichoke. As these are absolutely best when they are so hot you can barely put them in your mouth, this is one of those dishes that I get up to make when everyone is already seated and eating, a batch at a time.

This batter, which is adapted from a Paolo Petroni recipe for Tuscan 'peasant' batter, works well for a mixture of vegetables, including zucchini (courgette) sticks, slices of mushroom, onion rings and whatever else you like – cauliflower florets are wonderful fried like this. Petroni uses it for meat too, but I prefer crumbing meat for deep-frying.

SERVES 4

70 g (2½ oz) plain (all-purpose) flour
1 egg
1 tablespoon olive oil
60 ml (2 fl oz/¼cup) dry white wine
   (or a splash of grappa)
juice of ½ lemon
5–6 whole fresh artichokes
vegetable oil, for deep-frying

Prepare the batter at least 30 minutes before you want to begin frying. Combine the flour, egg, olive oil and white wine in a bowl and mix until just combined. Rest the batter in the fridge, covered, for at least 30 minutes, or until needed.

Fill a large bowl with cold water and squeeze the lemon juice into it (saving the lemon half) – this is to prevent the artichokes from oxidising, which they do quite quickly. Prepare the artichokes by first peeling the tough outer leaves off, one by one, from the bottom going around and up until you reach very pale-coloured, tender leaves. Cut off the stalk, leaving about 2–3 cm (¾–1¼ in) in length, then peel the base of the artichoke and the stub of stalk remaining. Rub the cut parts with the squeezed lemon half as you go. Cut the top, pointed half of the artichoke off completely

and discard. Place the artichokes in the lemon water until you have trimmed all the artichokes this way.

One by one, slice each artichoke in half vertically. If there is a fluffy, thistle-like choke, remove it with a teaspoon. Slice the flesh into eighths and place the artichoke pieces in the lemon water. Continue with the rest of the artichokes; they can be kept like this for several hours, or until needed.

When you're ready to fry, drain the artichoke slices very well, then pat dry with a tea towel (dish towel) or paper towels. Place a handful of artichoke pieces in the cold batter.

Heat enough vegetable oil in a deep, heavy-based saucepan over a medium–high heat to completely cover the artichoke pieces. The oil is hot enough when the bottom of a wooden spoon placed in it is immediately surrounded by tiny bubbles. Let any excess batter run off the artichoke pieces, then fry in batches in a single layer, turning for even cooking, for about 90 seconds in total.

Drain on paper towel and season with salt and pepper while hot. Serve immediately and keep topping up the plate with the rest of the artichokes as they are ready.

169

Insalata Russa

RUSSIAN SALAD

So-called 'Russian salad' (or Olivier salad as it is often known elsewhere) is a classic, even old-fashioned Tuscan favourite, appearing on family tables for basically every holiday from Easter to Christmas since the early 1900s as a side dish to important main dishes. This could also appear in Torino's chapter, as it is a popular addition to Piemontese antipasto platters.

I have to admit, I have not been a fan of *insalata russa*, finding most versions of it unappealing – with more mayonnaise (and not the home-made kind) than overcooked vegetables floating in it – until I finally tasted one at a friend's place in San Gimignano at Christmas – it was fresh and green, with just enough mayonnaise to hold the vegetables together. With just one mouthful I was convinced that *insalata russa* had the potential to be delicious.

When I researched old recipes for it, I noticed the ingredients were largely green vegetables (Artusi in 1891 includes diced beetroot and radicchio, so perhaps you could say magenta too) and a very small amount ('*qualche cucchiaino*' advises Ada Boni in 1929: a few teaspoons) of home-made mayonnaise, which I found perfect. Their recipes were also balanced with something acidic – pickles, lemon juice or vinegar (Boni calls for tarragon vinegar), which does a lot to pep it up. I like to add a spoonful of thick, plain yoghurt to the dressing (the only untraditional thing about this recipe) to cut through the mayonnaise and add some of that welcome acidity. How it reached the sticky, sweet, mayonnaise-filled mess you often find today I do not know, but please, let's bring back the version from a century ago.

Some additions to consider: one or two hard-boiled eggs, chopped or sliced; pickled onions (one of Nonna Lina's additions); thin, raw slices of crunchy cucumber; steamed or boiled carrot (which I prefer not to include as I find it too sweet here).

171

SERVES 4–6

2 medium potatoes

120 g (4½ oz) green beans, tops cut off and beans cut into 2–3 cm (¾–1¼ in) pieces

70 g (2½ oz) fresh or frozen peas

1 celery stalk, finely chopped

handful of fresh flat-leaf (Italian) parsley leaves, finely chopped

1½ tablespoons capers (if brined, drained; if preserved in salt, rinsed then soaked in clean water for 15 minutes, then drained)

4–5 cornichons, finely sliced

3 anchovy fillets preserved in oil, chopped

DRESSING

1–2 tablespoons mayonnaise

1 tablespoon thick natural yoghurt (like Greek yoghurt)

1 tablespoon extra-virgin olive oil

1 tablespoon red-wine vinegar

Rinse the potatoes and place them whole in their skins in a pot of cold water. Bring to the boil and cook until the potatoes are easily pierced with a fork. A few minutes before taking the potatoes out, add the green beans and peas.

Drain and let the vegetables cool. In the meantime, make the dressing by whisking the ingredients together in a small bowl. Season with salt and pepper to taste.

When cool, peel the potatoes and cut into 1 cm (½ in) cubes.

Toss the cooled, cooked vegetables and the rest of the ingredients together, then stir through the dressing, adjusting the seasoning to taste.

Cipolle al Forno

BAKED ONIONS

This is one of those extraordinarily satisfying things to make that requires very little effort – just time and heat – for maximum output. It was a side dish that was often made when the cast-iron wood stove happened to be on. A few onions, whole, and perhaps a few potatoes in their jackets too, would simply be slipped into the hot coals and ashes of the stove and left to cook until completely tender. When my mother-in-law Angela was growing up, it was usually on the menu for *Tutti i Santi*, All Saint's Day, on 1 November, along with chestnuts, toasted in a perforated pan over the fire, and roasted meat on skewers.

Angela remembers her family doing this just with red onions (they were all that were available in Tuscany until recent times) and it is still the family favourite, but it works with white or brown onions too. I tend to double the recipe; the leftovers are delicious cold and work very well in salads or sandwiches too – you can never make too much.

SERVES 4 AS A SIDE DISH

4 red onions in their skins
1 tablespoon red-wine vinegar
2 tablespoons extra-virgin olive oil

Preheat the oven to 180°C (350°F).

Place the onions in a baking dish and bake for 1 hour. The onions should be extremely tender and fragrant. Leave to cool slightly, then remove the base of the onion where the roots are, and the skins. Cut the cooked onion into quarters and dress with vinegar, olive oil, a pinch of salt and freshly ground black pepper.

173

Patate Schiacciate

SQUASHED POTATOES

These potatoes are somewhere between mashed and boiled, a dish that was often on the table to accompany meat dishes in Angela's family (often, each would do their own 'squashing' on their plate, with a fork and a good drizzle of extra-virgin olive oil). I like to finish them in a cast-iron frying pan (you can also put them in the oven) with plenty of olive oil to crisp and brown the outsides too. It is best to use small–medium potatoes for this. If you have very large ones, cut them into evenly sized chunks.

SERVES 4–6

800 g (1 lb 12 oz) floury potatoes, rinsed
  and peeled
60 ml (2 fl oz/¼ cup) extra-virgin olive oil,
  or as needed

Place the potatoes whole in a large saucepan of salted cold water and bring to the boil. Cook until the potatoes are easily pierced with a fork.

Drain the potatoes well, then, one by one, gently squash them with a spatula or the palm of your hand on a chopping board until they begin to break apart. Pour over the olive oil and sprinkle each with salt. You can serve them just like this or you can give them a crisp, golden-brown crust by placing them in a pan with a splash more olive oil. This takes about 5–7 minutes over a medium–high heat.

175

Pomarola di Nonna Lina

NONNA LINA'S FRESH TUSCAN TOMATO SAUCE

Pomarola is one of the traditions that encompasses everything we think about Italian food: family, seasonality, self-sufficiency and the splatter of tomato sauce. Making it is an age-old Tuscan late-summer activity, using a mix of San Marzano tomatoes (also known as Roma tomatoes), ribbed, flattened tomatoes known as Fiorentini and rounder Cuore di Bue (Bull's heart) tomatoes and *aromi*, 'aromas', which could simply mean basil, or the full trilogy of carrot, celery and onion. They are cooked together until the vegetables are entirely soft and giving, passed through a *passaverdura*, or food mill (see Note), then bottled and stored away for winter when tomatoes no longer taste as they should – or for those nights when all you have energy for is to boil some pasta and tip over some delicious tomato sauce, with a knob of butter like Nonna Lina would have served it.

The first time I volunteered to make the season's *pomarola* when no one else had time, Angela's eyes lit up and she immediately recounted to me her mother Lina's recipe – the one she would make every summer. She remembers all of Lina's recipes as if it were yesterday that she was watching intently from the sidelines: tomatoes (Lina would break them up with her hands), onion, carrot for sweetness, celery, parsley and a lot of basil. Sometimes, she would add the tiniest bit of sugar to counteract the acidity of the tomatoes. Olive oil, just a little, if you want. Oh yes, and some water, especially if the tomatoes aren't watery themselves.

MAKES ABOUT 2.5–3 KG (5½ LB–6 LB 10 OZ) SAUCE

4 kg (8 lb 13 oz) very ripe summer tomatoes
1 large red onion, roughly chopped
1 large carrot, roughly chopped
2 celery stalks with leaves, roughly chopped
½ bunch of flat-leaf (Italian) parsley, leaves only
½ bunch basil leaves, torn
extra-virgin olive oil, for topping up the jars

Wash the tomatoes well and chop them roughly, placing them directly into a very large stockpot (or two medium–large ones, if you don't have one big enough). Add the onion, carrot, celery and herbs and heat over a low–medium heat. As they warm, the tomatoes will begin to let out their juices. Season with salt – I would add a generous pinch taken with four fingers, but remember that you also have another opportunity to season according to taste later. You may need to help the tomatoes along by adding some water if they are not juicy enough – around 250 ml (8½ fl oz/1 cup) to start with.

Let the vegetables cook down gently, stirring occasionally. You should notice more and more liquid filling the pot. As soon as the vegetables are covered, turn the heat down to low and let it all simmer away gently for 40 minutes to 1 hour.

In the meantime, prepare jars for bottling. If you plan to use the pomarola right away, you can simply store the sauce in the fridge and use over the next few days. Preparing jars for bottling is much like jam making and canning – use large, clean, glass jars and clean lids that have been washed well with warm, soapy water and air-dried.

Taste the tomatoes and adjust with perhaps another pinch of salt if needed. If you think it is too acidic, you can add a pinch of sugar (Lina would have but I don't).

Remove from the heat and begin the food-mill process. Scoop out the vegetables, bit by bit, and pass them through a *passaverdura* (food mill; see Note) set over a large pot (or a bowl, but I find the mill is more likely to sit more obediently over a large pot). Every now and then,

when you have exhausted the leftover scraps in the food mill, discard these into the compost or bin, and carry on.

When the sauce is completely smooth, bring it back to a rolling boil over a high heat. If you feel the sauce needs to be reduced further, continue cooking until it is has thickened to the desired consistency, then distribute the hot sauce between jars. Pour a 3 mm (⅛ in) layer of olive oil over the top of the sauce before closing the lid tightly, and leave on your kitchen bench until the sauce has cooled and you hear that 'pop' of the lid sealing itself.

NOTE

A passaverdura *(a food mill or mouli) is a must in an Italian kitchen. I don't know how this could be done without the help of one; it manages to separate unwanted fibres, seeds and other bits, while at the same time it turns the vegetables into a silky, smooth sauce. A blender will not do the same job and passing the* pomarola *manually through a sieve would be tedious. It's not a fancy contraption, but rather old-fashioned and chunky, even awkward at times when trying to balance it above a bowl or a pot that isn't really the right size for its little legs. But, once you have one, you will see – you'll use it for everything: creamy sauces or soup, even jam (this was a revelation for me; no need to skin and pit your fruit, just pop it all in, the* passaverdura *does the rest).*

Pasta al Pomodoro Crudo

PASTA WITH RAW TOMATO SAUCE

This was one of Nonno Mario's dishes, something that Marco still loves to make for lunch on hot summer days. When you have really good, ripe summer tomatoes there is nothing more satisfying than enjoying them fresh. Here, they are chopped into a juicy sauce that is basically a cool dressing to coat pasta, so the result is not piping hot – a blessing during the sweltering Tuscan summer, not only to eat but also because you don't have to spend time in front of a hot stove other than to boil the pasta.

Patience Gray has a similar recipe in *Honey from a Weed* (page 65), though she adds a green chilli and doesn't want cheese in hers (me either, although sometimes I quite like tearing apart a fresh ball of buffalo mozzarella to add to the top of the pasta), while Jane Grigson in her *Vegetable Book* adds spring onions (scallions) and lets the tomatoes, in their dressing, marinate for three hours – suggestions that are worth experimenting with once you realise you want to eat this every day of the week. One thing I think is important to mention is that fresh tomatoes should be kept at room temperature when they are at their tastiest and best – don't store them in the fridge. If you can't help yourself, try to let them sit out of the fridge for half an hour before you use them.

Use any pasta shape you like; Marco remembers most often having this with *farfalle*, bow-tie pasta.

178

SERVES 4

1 kg (2 lb 3 oz) ripe tomatoes
1 garlic clove, finely chopped
handful fresh basil leaves, torn
2–3 tablespoons extra-virgin olive oil,
   plus extra for drizzling
320 g (11½ oz) your favourite pasta

Score a cross on the bottom of the tomatoes. Bring a large pot of water to boil (the one you will use for the pasta) and blanch the tomatoes for 30 seconds. Remove with a slotted spoon and immediately place them in a bowl of iced water. Once cool enough to handle, peel off the skins. Chop the tomatoes into quarters and scrape out and discard the seeds. Roughly chop the flesh and either leave as is (my preference) or, if you prefer a smooth sauce, you can pulse in a food processor, smash with a mortar and pestle or pass through a *passaverdura* (food mill).

Combine the tomatoes in a bowl with a good pinch of salt (taken with three fingers), the garlic, torn basil leaves (don't chop them with a knife, which leaves a black, oxidised edge; instead, rip them by hand) and the extra-virgin olive oil. Set aside until the pasta is ready (you can prepare this a couple of hours before you need it; just keep it in the fridge until 30 minutes before you want to serve it).

Bring the pot of water used to blanch the tomatoes back to the boil, salt appropriately (see page 17) and drop in the pasta. Cook until al dente. Drain and add the pasta to the bowl of tomatoes, tossing to coat. Serve immediately, perhaps with an extra drizzle of olive oil.

Mezze Maniche ai Pomodorini Gratinati

MEZZE MANICHE WITH ROASTED CHERRY TOMATOES

Tomatoes in pasta are very popular with my in-laws, who, over the generations, have always enjoyed them in every which way possible – from *pomarola*, to raw, to this baked gratin of sorts where the pasta is tipped right into the baking dish. I love this preparation too; it's like a very low-maintenance *pasta al pomodoro*, with the roasting turning up the tomato flavour a notch.

SERVES 4

2–3 teaspoons capers, rinsed
750 g (1 lb 11 oz) cherry tomatoes, halved
1 teaspoon dried oregano (or, if fresh, a few
   sprigs, leaves picked)
2 tablespoons extra-virgin olive oil, plus extra
   for serving if needed
30 g (1 oz) pecorino or parmesan, grated
320 g (11½ oz) mezze maniche (or other short
   pasta, such as penne)

Preheat the oven to 180°C (350°F) and bring a large pot of salted water to the boil (see page 17).

If using salted capers, after rinsing off the excess salt, soak them in fresh water for 10 minutes, then chop finely.

Place the cherry tomato halves in a baking dish (personally I go for a large, earthenware dish that can be presented at the table) and scatter over the capers and oregano, and pour over the olive oil. Sprinkle over some freshly ground black pepper and the pecorino (with the cheese and capers you likely won't need extra salt). Bake in the oven for 15–20 minutes, or until the tomatoes have become slumped and juicy and the pecorino is golden and melted. Remove from the oven.

While the tomatoes are baking, boil the pasta until al dente. Drain, reserving about 60 ml (2 fl oz/¼ cup) of the pasta cooking water. Tip the drained pasta directly into the baking dish with the tomatoes and stir to combine, adding some of the pasta cooking water and a splash more olive oil, if needed. Take the baking dish to the table and serve immediately.

179

Pasta al Forno di Angela

ANGELA'S LASAGNE

This is Angela's signature dish, and one she really does well. It's the one most requested by her grandchildren and it is the one she'll prepare for every family gathering, in colossal aluminium trays. She never measures anything and, as a result, always makes double the amount actually needed and the fridge will be full of the ingredients needed to make several more trays for the days that follow. But it's all part of the ritual of her *pasta al forno*.

There's a rhythm to the making of *pasta al forno*, or lasagne. There's the sugo, the meat sauce, which has to be made the day before. Angela sets her two largest pots on the stove and makes industrial quantities of it. Then there's the béchamel. Marco will often argue over the quality of the milk she uses to make it with, urging her to use fresh milk. She uses store-bought fresh lasagne sheets and store-bought, pre-ground parmesan to make life easier (her job in the kitchen growing up was always to grate the cheese and, since her family was one that loved plenty of cheese, she had to grate, grate, grate), and fresh mozzarella, which she tears up with her hands.

Then it's an assembly line. First, some sugo across the bottom of the tray. Then a layer of pasta. More sugo, generous swathes of it. Béchamel, quite fluid, strategically blobbed all over, then stirred right into the layer of sugo and mixed together into a creamy, rusty-pink sauce.

Then the torn mozzarella goes on, here and there, followed by a dusting of grated parmesan, and so on until the tray is full. It's baked until it's bubbling and crisp and, since it's usually being taken to someone's house, it's done well in advance. This, I believe, is part of the secret to the success of a good pasta al forno: that time where the whole thing settles and the flavours mingle, and then it is most likely reheated, so the edges get extra crunchy – the best bit.

I watch her as she does it and she says, without even looking up, 'Whenever I make *pasta al forno*, even now, I have her here next to me'. Lina, that is. Right up until her old age, Lina was in the kitchen, cooking for her daughter and her grown grandchildren. When she was so frail she could finally no longer keep up with the cooking, she had Angela do it but she would insist on sitting in – or rather, standing, propped up against the corner of the kitchen table – overseeing everything, instructing. Still cooking, really: 'You missed a spot there. You need a bit more sugo here.' When Angela would try to send her to bed, Lina would shake her head and say she'd rather keep her company and participate in the cooking.

SERVES 6–8

MEAT SAUCE

1 onion, finely chopped
½ celery stalk, finely chopped
¼ carrot, finely chopped
1 garlic clove, finely chopped
1 rosemary sprig, leaves picked and
   finely chopped
a few whole sage leaves
handful of flat-leaf (Italian) parsley leaves,
   finely chopped
80–100 ml (2⅓–3½ fl oz) extra-virgin
   olive oil
600 g (1 lb 5 oz) minced (ground) beef
300 g (10½ oz) minced (ground) pork
400 ml (13½ fl oz) white wine
600 g (1 lb 5 oz) tomato passata
   (puréed tomatoes)

BÉCHAMEL

50 g (1¾ oz) butter
40 g (1½ oz) plain (all-purpose) flour
500 ml (17 fl oz/2 cups) full-cream (whole)
   milk, warmed
freshly ground white pepper

PASTA

300 g (10½ oz) plain (all-purpose) flour,
   plus extra for dusting if needed
3 eggs

TO ASSEMBLE

150 g (5½ oz/1½ cups) grated parmesan
   or Grana Padano
250 g (9 oz) mozzarella

Prepare the meat sauce at least a day in advance, if possible. Cook the onion, celery, carrot and garlic with the herbs and olive oil in a large saucepan over a medium heat. Add a good pinch of salt and cook until the vegetables are soft, about 10 minutes. Add the minced beef and pork and cook, stirring frequently, until the meat becomes evenly opaque, about 7 minutes. Add another pinch of salt, pour over the wine and increase the heat to high. Cook, stirring occasionally, until the liquid is reduced significantly, about 15 minutes.

Add the passata and 600 ml (20½ fl oz) water. Add another good pinch of salt and freshly ground black pepper. Bring the sauce to the boil, reduce the heat to low and simmer very gently for at least 1 hour, uncovered. Check on it occasionally, stirring. It should reduce into a slightly thickened, fragrant sauce. Taste for seasoning and adjust to your liking. Set aside. If doing this in advance, transfer the sauce to an airtight container, leave to cool completely and refrigerate until needed.

For the béchamel, heat the butter and flour in a saucepan over a low–medium heat and, once the butter has melted, stir together for a couple of minutes until you have a thick paste-like mixture. Slowly whisk in the warm milk (a little at a time at first), whisking until the milk is incorporated and smooth. Cook the béchamel for about 10 minutes, stirring often, until thickened. The sauce should coat the back of a spoon easily but it doesn't need to be too thick – Angela keeps hers fairly liquid. Season with salt and white pepper (grated nutmeg is more traditional, but the family prefers pepper). Set aside. You can also do this in advance and store in the refrigerator for up to 3 days.

For the pasta, sift the flour into a bowl and create a well in the middle. Crack the eggs into the well and begin stirring with a fork, first to break up the eggs, then, once well-beaten, begin incorporating the flour until you have a thick and sticky mixture.

Use your hands to finish combining the eggs with as much flour as they can take to result in a smooth, elastic dough – you may or may not need all of the flour, which is why this technique of slowly incorporating the flour is used. It shouldn't be sticky either but, if it is, you can dust with more flour. Knead on a lightly floured surface for a few minutes, then cover in plastic wrap and let the dough rest for 30 minutes.

Cut the dough into three portions and, working one portion at a time, dust the piece of dough and run it through a pasta machine, going from the thickest to thinnest or second-thinnest setting (depending on the machine), about 1 mm (1⁄16 in) thick. If you need to, dust the dough with extra flour between settings. Cut the long pieces of dough into convenient lengths that fit the dish you are planning to use for baking and set aside, preferably on a lightly-floured surface, until needed.

When you're ready to assemble the lasagne, preheat the oven to 180°C (350°F) and bring a large pot of salted water to the boil. Blanch the pasta sheets for 1 minute each, then drain with a slotted spoon and place on a clean, damp tea towel (dish towel) – be careful not to overlap the pasta sheets as they stick easily.

Just before assembling the lasagne, reheat the meat sauce as it will be easier to layer and stir through the béchamel.

In a glass or ceramic rectangular casserole dish, assemble the following layers: first, a thin layer of sauce on the bottom of the dish, then a single layer of par-boiled pasta sheets, another layer of sauce, a handful of parmesan and some torn pieces of mozzarella dotted here and there. Continue layering pasta, sauce and cheese, ending in a layer of cheese.

Bake for 15–20 minutes, or until golden brown and bubbling. Leave to rest for at least 15 minutes before serving.

NOTE

You can use store-bought lasagne sheets; Angela always does (you'll need 400–500 g/ 14 oz–1 lb 2 oz fresh pasta sheets). But, if you'd like to try your hand at making the pasta sheets fresh, they're so easy to make if you have a pasta rolling machine and, in my opinion, worth the extra effort. This easily serves six generous portions (ideal if this is all you're having), or eight normal portions for a meal that will probably have several courses. When Angela makes a bigger tray for a family gathering to serve twelve, she simply doubles the béchamel and adds a little more mozzarella to make it stretch.

If I may add a slight grammatical deviation: yes, lasagne is written and pronounced with an 'e' on the end. As with most pasta, lasagne is plural. Lasagna with an 'a' is singular, as in one sheet of lasagna. It'd be like saying 'spaghetto' when in fact you mean 'spaghetti'.

THREE GENERATIONS
OF TORTELLINI

Eating tortellini, for Marco, is akin to time-travelling. As for so many Tuscans, tortellini were a fixture on his family's Sunday table, and really for any special occasion – Christmas or Easter, especially. Usually they were served with sugo, a rich Tuscan meat sauce, Nonna Lina's specialty – she had a very particular way of making her sugo, with whole pieces of beef rather than mince (see page 192) – or in beef broth (see page 205), a delicate and warming dish, always a comfort.

My mother-in-law Angela also recounts eating them often. Sometime in the 1950s, when Angela was a young child, her father Mario began making them to serve on New Year's Eve at the neighbourhood bar that Angela's grandfather owned. Lina would make the sugo, of course, but Mario would put it all together and serve them at midnight to ring in the New Year together with cheap spumante and a round of tombola (bingo). It started a trend. All the bars in town began doing it too and, up until the 1970s when parties became a more popular way of celebrating, you could still find tortellini at midnight on New Year's Eve in the bars around Fucecchio. I think it's a tradition worth keeping.

Tortellini may belong to Emilia-Romagna (its cities Bologna and Modena are contenders for the city of origin of what is arguably Italy's most famous filled pasta), which borders Tuscany to the north, but they hold a special place in the hearts and kitchens of many Tuscans. One taste of *tortellini in brodo* (in chicken or beef broth) or tortellini covered in sugo will send ripples of childhood memories of Sunday lunches with nonna to most Tuscans – and because of this, they continue to appear in the most homely and traditional of Tuscan trattorie.

The filling is one of meat and salumi and will change from household to household, although in 1974 the 'Confraternity of the Tortellino' defined the 'original' recipe as being made up of roasted pork loin, prosciutto, mortadella di Bologna, parmesan, eggs and nutmeg. Pellegrino Artusi, in 1891, used bone marrow in place of the pork and Ada Boni, in 1929, added veal, turkey breast and lamb's brains to the mortadella, prosciutto and parmesan. The truth is, this is another dish that works well with leftover meat – if you already have some leftover roasted pork, turkey or beef, you can use that in place of the pork loin in the recipe on page 187 (100 g/3½ oz is fine, if already cooked).

Tortellini al Sugo

TORTELLINI WITH MEAT SAUCE

This is Marco's preferred way of making sugo, or meat sauce. I love that the tradition of sugo in his family runs strong, and that a member of each generation has his or her own way of doing it, inspired by the previous ones. His Nonna Lina's meat sauce (page 192) was made with whole pieces of meat rather than mince. His mother Angela's sugo (see pages 180–3) is inspired by years of watching her mother Lina make her sugo, but for convenience she uses mince, and a mixture of beef with a small amount of pork. When she is really busy, she has no shame in using pre-cut frozen onions or blending all the vegetables in a food processor rather than chopping them with a mezzaluna as Nonna Lina would have painstakingly done. Marco too likes to use minced (ground) beef and pork, though in equal amounts that are roasted thoroughly in the pan to bring out the flavour – and he is heavy handed with the wine (of course).

SERVES 6

MARCO'S SUGO

3 tablespoons olive oil
250 g (9 oz) minced (ground) beef
 (preferably not too lean)
250 g (9 oz) minced (ground) pork
 (preferably not too lean)
1 carrot, finely chopped
1 small onion, finely chopped
½ celery stalk, finely chopped
1 tablespoon tomato paste
 (concentrated purée)
400 ml (13½ fl oz) dry red wine
400 g (14 oz) tomato passata
 (puréed tomatoes)

FILLING

30 g (1 oz) butter
1 rosemary sprig
1 garlic clove
150 g (5½ oz) pork loin, diced
100 g (3½ oz) prosciutto, roughly chopped
100 g (3½ oz) mortadella, roughly chopped
100 g (3½ oz) parmesan, finely grated, plus
 extra to serve
1 whole egg
freshly grated nutmeg

PASTA

300 g (10½ oz/2 cups) plain (all-purpose) flour,
 plus extra for dusting
3 eggs

To make the sugo, heat 1 tablespoon of the olive oil in a wide, deep pan over a high heat. Marco likes to brown the meat very well, like you would a steak. This means you can brown it in very small batches or do it in one batch, wait for the meat to release all its liquid, then continue cooking it until it is a deep brown. It will pop and crackle as it gets to this stage. It takes about 15–20 minutes over a high heat.

Once the meat is properly browned (don't worry about anything stuck to the bottom of the pan; this will add flavour), turn the heat right down to low and add the vegetables, along with the rest of the olive oil and a three-fingered pinch of salt and some freshly ground black pepper. Cook gently until the vegetables soften, about 10–15 minutes. Add the tomato paste, turn the heat up to medium–high and cook for 2 minutes. Pour in the wine and bring to a lively simmer, then let it cook down until the wine is almost all evaporated, about 10 minutes.

Pour in the passata, along with about 125 ml (4 fl oz/½ cup) water and another good pinch of salt and freshly ground black pepper. Reduce the heat to the lowest setting – even the smallest hob if necessary – so that it can simmer slowly, covered, for at least 2 hours; 3 is plenty. Uncover the pot for the last 30 minutes so that the sauce can reduce and thicken slightly. Taste for seasoning and adjust as needed.

For the filling, heat the butter, rosemary and garlic in a frying pan over a medium heat until the butter melts and the garlic begins to sizzle. Add the pork, tossing through the butter to coat, and continue cooking until the meat is cooked through, about 5–7 minutes. Let cool. Remove the pork from the pan, discarding the butter, rosemary and garlic.

Place the cooled pork, the prosciutto and mortadella in a food processor and blend until broken up into tiny pieces. Add the parmesan, egg and nutmeg and continue blending until you have a smooth, paste-like filling. Set aside, preferably to chill in the fridge if you are preparing this well in advance.

Make the pasta by sifting the flour into a wide bowl and making a well in the middle. Crack the eggs in and begin beating the eggs with a fork, slowly incorporating the flour around them until the mixture becomes creamy and then, eventually, too stiff to continue using a fork. With your hands, continue the same procedure, mixing the eggs with the flour slowly, until you have a soft and elastic dough (you might not need to use all the flour). Doing it slowly allows the flour to absorb all the liquid properly. Cover the dough with plastic wrap and chill in the fridge for at least 30 minutes.

To build the tortellini I like to work a bit at a time. Divide the dough into four pieces. Roll out a piece of the dough (keeping the others covered so they do not dry out) to the thinnest setting on a pasta machine (you can dust lightly with flour as needed, but try not to use too much as it dries the pasta out and prevents it from sealing together). Place the pasta sheet on a lightly floured surface and, with a smooth pastry cutter, pizza cutter or a sharp knife, cut the dough into squares measuring about 3.5–4 cm (1½ in) each side.

Place small, pea-sized (or no bigger than chickpea-sized) balls of filling in the centre of each pasta square, fold in half to create a triangle, pressing the edges gently to seal (see Notes).

With the folded edge facing downwards and the point towards the ceiling, slightly push the ball of filling inwards, then use the tip of your index finger (or your pinky if you have big hands like Marco) to help hold the shape of the tortellino while you bring the two outer corners together to meet, then press to seal. Place the finished tortellini on a tray or large wooden board lined with baking paper. Continue with the rest – rolling a portion of the pasta and filling and forming the tortellini – until finished. If you're not cooking the tortellini right away, you can leave them like this, lightly covered with a clean tea towel (dish towel) – they can now be left to dry out slightly – in the refrigerator or a cool, dry place until the next day.

Heat a large pot of boiling, salted water (see page 17) and heat the sugo while you are waiting for the water to come to the boil. Drop the tortellini into the boiling water and cook until they float and the pasta is al dente, about 3–4 minutes, then drain.

Serve in shallow bowls with the sugo over the top and grated parmesan, if desired.

187

NOTES

You can make all the elements of this dish ahead of time. In fact, many would argue that both the filling and the sugo are best made one day (at least) in advance, giving the flavours time to build up and get to know each other. Even if you're attempting to tackle this all in one day, I would definitely do it in the following order: sugo, filling, pasta. You can also serve tortellini simply in butter or in chicken or beef broth (see page 205). In this case, this recipe will still make four to five generous serves. With the sugo, and especially if you are serving this as part of a multi-course meal, you can easily stretch it to six good portions.

When sealing the tortellini, I try to do this a bit at a time, keeping any waiting sheets of pasta covered loosely with plastic wrap and a tea towel. If you find the pasta has dried out a little, you can brush the edges with a small amount of water, but if it dries out too much you will not be able to form the tortellini, so I suggest working a bit at a time, keeping all pasta covered, until you get into a good rhythm.

188

Sugo di Carne di Nonna Lina

NONNA LINA'S MEAT SAUCE

Nonna Lina was a pedantic cook, easily worried about things like the shelf life of freshly cut prosciutto slices or just-made crema. Even the freshest fish had to be used that day. Another hang-up she had was about minced (ground) meat. She was suspicious and untrusting of it, feeling its quality was always compromised. Instead, she preferred to make her sugo with cuts of meat that she was familiar with – a cut from the rump that, in Tuscany, is known as *bicchiere*, usually – which she would cook whole, in slices, directly in the sugo, and then chop finely herself afterwards. If she had one, she would often add a sausage, too.

According to Paolo Petroni – whose book, *Il Grande Libro della Vera Cucina Toscana* (which contains more than one hundred Tuscan recipes) is another classic household favourite – this is the true way to make a Tuscan sugo: with whole pieces of beef or veal. This is what makes the difference between a Tuscan 'sugo' and an Emilian 'ragù'. He notes, too, that you can make a delicious rabbit sauce the same way – in Tuscany, this is why rabbit is sold whole at the butcher, complete with the head. It all goes in the pot (for flavour) then, afterwards, the meat is pulled off the bone, chopped and put back in the sauce and the bones and head are discarded.

SERVES 6–8
AS A FIRST COURSE WITH PASTA

750 g (1 lb 11 oz) boneless beef ribs, sliced
1 pork and fennel sausage (optional)
60 ml (2 fl oz/1/4 cup) extra-virgin olive oil
1 large onion, finely chopped
½ carrot, finely chopped
½ celery stalk, finely chopped
1 garlic clove, finely chopped
a few sprigs each of sage, flat-leaf (Italian)
    parsley, basil and rosemary
250 ml (8½ fl oz/1 cup) white wine
330 g (11½ oz) tomato passata (puréed
    tomatoes)
330 ml (11 fl oz) vegetable or beef stock

Sprinkle the beef with a couple of pinches of salt and freshly ground black pepper and remove the casing of the sausage, if using. Set aside.

Heat the olive oil in a large casserole pot over a low heat. Gently cook the onion, carrot, celery, garlic and herbs with a three-fingered pinch of salt for about 10 minutes, or until softened. Add the

beef and crumble over the sausage, if using, then increase the heat to medium and cook for about 15 minutes, or until the meat is opaque. Add the wine, increase the heat to high and bring it to a lively simmer. Cook for 7–10 minutes, or until the wine is almost entirely reduced. Pour in the passata, add another pinch of salt and some pepper, along with the stock and bring to the boil. Reduce the heat to low and simmer for 1 hour, uncovered, topping up with water as necessary if the liquid is reducing too quickly.

Lina would have transferred the meat to her chopping board and then cut it into tiny pieces with the mezzaluna. A less messy option is to pulse it in a food processor until reduced to tiny pieces, then return to the pan, stirring to combine well. Check for seasoning and adjust as you like.

This could be used for lasagne (see pages 180–3), for tortellini (see pages 187–8) or simply for enjoying with your favourite pasta – bucatini were Nonno Mario's preference.

Minestrone dell'Orto

VEGETABLE PATCH MINESTRONE

Soup, or *minestra*, has long had an important place on Tuscan tables. A vegetable minestrone would be the typical meal on fasting days leading up to big Catholic holidays like Easter Friday and Christmas Eve – or, traditionally, simply on Fridays in general when meat was avoided and either fish or vegetables took centre stage.

Minestrone is such an adaptable soup recipe, but the idea is to take advantage of the freshest seasonal ingredients springing out of the vegetable patch (or appearing in the farmers' market) rather than looking at it as an opportunity to clear out the sad-looking scraps at the bottom of the crisper drawer in the fridge. This recipe is my favourite minestrone, but merely a suggestion to work from. Use fresh peas, artichokes or asparagus in spring; basil, zucchini (courgettes) and fresh rather than tinned beans in the summer; pumpkin (squash) in the autumn, and root vegetables and dark leafy greens in winter. You can use chickpeas, lentils or cannellini beans in place of the borlotti (cranberry) beans. Leave out the pancetta to keep it vegetarian, if desired. If you want to make this more substantial, you can use beef broth (see page 205) rather than vegetable stock. If you want something lighter, you can also leave out the starchy things, such as the beans, pasta or farro.

193

TUSCANY

SERVES 6

2–3 tablespoons extra-virgin olive oil,
   plus extra for drizzling
3 slices pancetta, chopped
a few sprigs of flat-leaf (Italian) parsley, stalks
   and leaves roughly chopped
2 garlic cloves, one finely chopped,
   one left whole
1 small onion, finely chopped
1 medium carrot, chopped
½ celery stalk, chopped
2 fresh or dried bay leaves
1 small potato, cut into 1 cm (½ in) dice
2 big handfuls of greens (cabbage, spinach,
   silverbeet/Swiss chard), rinsed and
   roughly chopped
125 g (4½ oz) peas
1 zucchini (courgette), cut into 1 cm (½ in) dice
1 x 400 g (14 oz) tin cooked borlotti (cranberry)
   beans, drained
200 g (7 oz) tinned whole, peeled tomatoes
   (or 2–3 ripe Roma tomatoes), roughly chopped
1 litre (34 fl oz/4 cups) vegetable stock
50 g (1¾ oz) small soup pasta (such as risoni,
   stelline) or farro
toasted bread for each bowl (optional)
finely grated parmesan, to serve (optional)

Heat the olive oil in a large stockpot over a low heat and add the pancetta, parsley and chopped garlic. Cook gently for 1–2 minutes. Add the onion, carrot, celery and bay leaves, along with a generous pinch of salt and some freshly ground black pepper, and continue cooking until the onion begins to become translucent and soft but not coloured, about 10 minutes. Add a splash of water or vegetable stock if the vegetables seem to stick or the onion begins to colour.

Add the rest of the vegetables, the beans, tomato and the stock. The vegetables should be covered but, if not, add some water to cover. Increase the heat to medium and bring to an active (but not furious) simmer and cook, uncovered, for about 30 minutes, or until the stock has reduced slightly and the vegetables are tender (note that certain vegetables are more delicate and require a shorter cooking time – for example peas, asparagus, spinach; you may prefer to add these towards the end of the cooking time along with the pasta). Drop in the pasta for about the last 10 minutes of the cooking time (the farro can go in from the beginning). Check for seasoning and adjust as you like.

Serve the minestrone with a piece of toasted bread (rubbed with the whole garlic clove if you like) in the bottom of the bowl and sprinkle over some grated parmesan, if desired, and a drizzle of extra-virgin olive oil.

NOTE

I always like to add the hard rind of parmesan when you can no longer grate anything else from it; I keep a stock of them in my freezer. It adds lovely flavour and, when it's softened after simmering in the soup, you can eat it, too. If you have one, throw it in.

BEN VENGA IL MINESTRONE

Pellegrino Artusi opens his recipe for minestrone with possibly my favourite anecdote in his 790-recipe cookbook (see pages 220–1). It is a dish that brings back bad memories for him. In 1885, Artusi visited the Tuscan port city of Livorno while a deadly cholera outbreak was snaking its way through the Italian peninsula. Poking his head into a nearby trattoria, he asks what the day's soup is. 'Minestrone' comes the reply. '*Ben venga il minestrone*,' says Artusi: welcome the minestrone.

That night, while sleeping in his hotel in Piazza del Voltone kept by a certain Signor Domenici, he begins to feel what he amusingly describes as a terrifying 'revolution' in his body and spends the night going back and forth to the bathroom, blaming the *maledetto* (damned) minestrone. He cuts his trip short, escaping to Florence on the first train the next day, only to discover the news that the epidemic had reached Livorno and that Domenici, his host, had been the city's first cholera victim. A close shave.

In his minestrone, Artusi recommends making *lesso* for a good beef broth (see page 205) and he likes a combination of green beans, cabbage, spinach and silverbeet (Swiss chard), along with the beans, rice, some prosciutto or pork rind and tomato paste (concentrated purée).

Arselle in Umido

<u>**WEDGE CLAM STEW**</u>

Maybe it's the port-city genes, but shellfish have always been loved in this family, by Marco and his Nonno Mario especially. This is a Tuscan preparation for beautiful, tiny, tasty wedge clams, also known as *arselle* or *telline*, which, when Marco was a child, his father Carlo used to collect on the beach, raking through the soft, wet sand. They are hard to find these days (and gone are the days when you were allowed to collect them on the beach) but, when we do spot them at the fishmonger, they are a real treat. You can use regular *vongole veraci* or even mussels instead.

Nonna Lina would have painstakingly removed all the meat from the tiny shells before serving, so no one had to get their hands dirty – this is something ingrained in Marco, who prefers to do this too, but I don't mind dealing with the shells while eating one bit.

This should be devoured with more bread than you can imagine.

<u>**SERVES 4**</u>

500 g (1 lb 2 oz) wedge clams (see Note)
1 ripe tomato (or 2 if it's not so juicy)
80 ml (2½ fl oz/⅓ cup) extra-virgin olive oil
1 garlic clove, finely chopped
125 ml (4 fl oz/½ cup) dry white wine
handful of flat-leaf (Italian) parsley,
    finely chopped
1 small hot red chilli, finely chopped
toasted crusty bread, to serve

Rinse the clams quickly under water and weed out any with crushed shells (a tiny chip or crack is usually fine) or any that are open and don't move when touched or squeezed.

Purge the clams, if necessary, for at least 1 hour. To do this, place in a large, preferably shallow, non-reactive (glass or ceramic) bowl. Cover the clams with 2–3 cm (¾ in–1¼ in) of saltwater (ideally use 35 g/1¼ oz of sea salt, not table salt, per 1 litre (34 fl oz/4 cups) of water to replicate the salinity of seawater – freshwater will kill them). To drain the clams, pick them up with your hands or a slotted spoon and transfer to a colander rather than tip them out (you will end up pouring any purged sand back onto them if you

do this). Give them another once over, checking especially for closed clams that could be dead and empty, holding nothing but a shell full of sand – these you especially do not want to find in your sauce! (An energetic shake, or tapping of clams on a chopping board will reveal the duds.) Live, healthy clams will stay tightly shut when moved around.

Score the bottom of the tomato with a cross and blanch for 30 seconds in boiling water, then plunge into ice-cold water. The skin should now be easy to peel off. Dice the tomato and place in a bowl with half of the olive oil and a pinch of salt (remember that the clams will let out a very flavourful liquid tasting of the sea as well). Set aside to marinate while preparing the clams.

Heat the rest of the olive oil in a frying pan over a medium heat and sizzle the garlic for a minute. Add the drained clams, toss and douse with the white wine. Continue cooking, turning up to a high heat and tossing to allow the clams room to open (discard any that don't). Add the parsley, chilli, the tomato and all its juices, give it another quick toss for a minute, then remove from the heat. Serve the clams with all the juices over toasted crusty bread.

NOTE

*If you are using real arselle, they have a
reputation for being very sandy no matter what
you do as they live in the finest sand possible.
If you're sourcing them from a fishmonger and
you're not sure, just ask if they have already been
purged and you can skip that step after rinsing
and going through them for any dead clams.*
*If you are using other clams and/or you have
bought your clams in a supermarket, they are
likely to be ready to go – just rinse and go through
them very well in case there are any closed dead
ones hoarding a shell full of sand.*

Totani al Piatto

STEAMED CALAMARI

This wonderful, easy dish, like the *Bracioline al burro* (page 213), was another invention of Nonna Lina's to satisfy young Marco's pickiness at the table – it, too, became a much-loved family staple that we continue to make at home. It is nothing more than very simply steamed calamari, inspired by a similar way of preparing sole. Since Lina's *batterie de cuisine* was rustic at best and consisted mostly of a huge array of mismatched pots with no lids, she would use a dinner plate placed strategically over a pot of boiling water to cook the calamari and another, inverted, on top to cover it.

Over the years, we have added to this dish with some fresh chilli and lemon juice, but feel free to leave this off if you are also cooking for picky eaters.

SERVES 4

800 g (1 lb 12 oz) whole calamari (see Note)
2 tablespoons olive oil
juice of 1 lemon
1 fresh hot red chilli, chopped (optional)
handful of flat-leaf (Italian) parsley, chopped
  (optional)
crusty bread, to serve

If you are working with whole calamari, you will have to clean them yourself first. Pull out the head, which should bring with it all of the interior, including the ink sac and quill (you may have to dig a little with your fingers to pry off the bits at the bottom). Pull off the fins/wings that are attached at the bottom of the body and, with these off, you should be able to peel off the skin. Slice down one side of the body so that you have one large, flat piece. Rinse and pat dry, then set aside. Now to deal with the head – cut just below the eyes so that the tentacles are still attached. Push out the beak, which you will find in the middle of the tentacles. Pull any hard bits off the suction cups by running the tentacles, one by one, through thumb and forefinger (if they are very stubborn you can also cut them off or run the blade of a sharp knife along them). Rinse and pat dry.

Place the calamari in a shallow pan (or, as Lina did, on a large dinner plate with a slightly raised edge), overlapping as needed. Dress the calamari with the olive oil, lemon juice, chilli (if using) and add a pinch of salt.

Place the pan/plate over a bain-marie (double boiler), such as a saucepan with a diameter slightly smaller than the pan or plate holding the calamari, partially filled with simmering water. Place a large lid (or another plate, inverted) over the top of the calamari and cook for for 30 minutes over a medium heat, or until the calamari are opaque, tender when pierced with a fork and have released an incredibly tasty, saucy liquid. Remove from the heat and rest the calamari for 10 minutes, covered. Serve sprinkled with parsley (if using), and, ideally, with plenty of crusty bread for mopping up the juices.

NOTE

In Italy, calamari are usually sold whole and uncleaned by weight. You can ask your fishmonger to clean them if you want to. If you are buying already cleaned calamari tubes, you only need 500 g (1 lb 2 oz) for this recipe.

Triglie alla Livornese

LIVORNO-STYLE WHOLE RED MULLET

Since the 60s Marco's grandparents have had a beachfront apartment near Livorno, which has been part of a ritual getaway every summer. One of the characteristics of Livorno's rustic seafood cuisine is the pairing of red wine with fish, both for drinking and cooking with. This is probably one of the best ways you can prepare red mullet – it is a firm family favourite.

Red mullet is a popular, very delicate and flaky fish that can be found year-round in Italy, but they are at their best between September and December. You find two different varieties of red mullet, known as *triglie di fango* (*mullus barbatus*) and *triglie di scoglio* (*mullus surmuletus*), named for their preferred hangout – muddy and sandy bottoms, or the rocky coastline. You can tell the difference between them for the brighter colours and defined stripes of the *triglie di scoglio* (in fact, it is known as striped red mullet in English, even though the two varieties are often not distinguished), which is tastier and, as it happens, more expensive – it easily reaches prices higher than prized Chianina beef in Tuscany. You can often find really small red mullets (about 12 cm/4¾ in in length) that are fried whole or used for tasty fish soups, but try to look for slightly bigger ones for this dish (about 18–20 cm/7–8 in long) that can still fit in a pan whole. You will get maximum flavour out of using whole fish, however you could also do this with just the fillets.

SERVES 4

4 whole red mullets, approx. 18–20 cm (7–8 in) long, gutted and scaled
3 tablespoons extra-virgin olive oil, plus extra for drizzling
1 garlic clove, squashed
1 fresh, small red chilli, finely chopped
1 x 400 g (14 oz) tin chopped tomatoes
125 ml (4 fl oz/½ cup) dry red wine, such as sangiovese
handful of flat-leaf (Italian) parsley, roughly chopped
crusty bread, to serve

Snip the fins off the mullets and rinse the fish gently, pat dry and sprinkle both sides with salt. Set aside.

In a pan large enough to hold the four mullets, slowly heat the olive oil and garlic over a low heat, infusing the oil for about 5 minutes, or until the garlic begins to become fragrant but is not yet coloured. Add the chilli and the tomatoes to the pan, along with a splash of water. Increase the heat to medium and cook for a few minutes, then add the red wine. Bring to a lively simmer, then place the mullet in a single layer in the pan and cook for about 3 minutes on each side, being careful not to break the delicate fish while flipping them over. Remove from the heat, sprinkle over the fresh parsley and serve with an extra drizzle of olive oil and good, crusty bread.

Cotolette d'Agnello Fritte

DEEP-FRIED LAMB CHOPS

This is a dish that only comes out once a year – for Easter. My in-laws, like many Tuscans, mostly have it on the menu out of pure tradition, but spring is also the only time of the year that you get proper lamb in Tuscany, even though it is easier now than it was a few years ago to find it a little outside the season. When I experienced my first Italian lamb, I realised it was proper, milk-fed lamb – the chops are so small they're like lollipops once cooked and you can finish them in one big bite.

These crunchy *cotolette* are always served with a lemon wedge and Deep-fried battered artichokes (page 169), usually following a course of Angela's *Pasta al forno di* (pages 180–3) and preceding a huge, trifle-like *Zuppa Inglese* (page 227). The cousins like to marinate their lamb chops in white wine overnight before the crumbing, but I find this completely disguises the flavour of the lamb (I believe this is actually why they do it, which makes you wonder why eat the lamb at all? The answer is: tradition).

My own Australian grandmother used to make something very similar, except that immediately after frying the crumbed cutlets she would then stew and soak them in a rich and chunky tomato and onion sauce, which reminds me so much of the preferred Tuscan way of reinventing leftover meat (especially crumbed and fried meat, which soaks up sauce like a sponge), such as the *Polpette di lesso* (see page 207) – and it is exactly how you should prepare any of these cutlets that remain as leftovers (see page 205).

202

SERVES 4

8 small lamb chops
2 eggs
125 g (4½ oz/1¼ cups) dried breadcrumbs
250 ml (8½ fl oz/1 cup) vegetable oil, for frying
lemon wedges, for serving

Remove the lamb chops from the fridge about 30 minutes before you are ready to cook them and inspect the lamb chops to see if any fat needs to be trimmed off.

Crack one of the eggs and place in a shallow bowl and beat lightly with a pinch of salt and some freshly ground black pepper. In another shallow bowl or plate, place the breadcrumbs.

Dip a lamb chop completely in the egg mixture to coat and then in the breadcrumbs, pressing well to ensure the crumbs stick, then place on a separate plate. Continue with the rest of the chops until they are all covered – if you run out of the egg mixture, crack the second egg and season as before.

Heat the oil in a wide frying pan over a medium–high heat. The oil will be ready when a cube of bread thrown in turns golden brown in about 15 seconds. Fry the lamb chops in a single layer, in batches, cooking for 6–8 minutes for medium-rare, or 10 minutes for medium, turning halfway through, until deep golden brown. Drain on paper towels as they are ready and sprinkle with salt while they are still hot. Serve immediately with lemon wedges.

NOTE

If you are preparing a larger serving than this, you may need to replenish the oil (especially if you find you have burnt crumbs at the bottom of the pan) between batches.

Roast Beef all'Inglese

ENGLISH-STYLE ROAST BEEF

Roast beef or, as it is often known in Italian, *rosbiffe*, is commonly offered in trattorie or delis around Florence. It most often presents itself as very thin slices of rosy-cheeked rare beef with generous spoonfuls of pan juices mixed with olive oil, to be eaten with a good amount of Tuscan bread and perhaps a salad or some twice-cooked greens, perfumed with garlic. Artusi mentions two different recipes for it in his cookbook (see pages 220–1), suggesting a cut such as sirloin for this roast. As this is such a simple recipe, I cannot stress how important it is to choose a good-quality piece of meat from a reputable source. Artusi prefers to cook his on the stovetop rather than roast in the oven – most Tuscans I know do too, some simply browning the meat and resting it, stopping there. But I find the oven reliable, which is what I want with a good roast beef.

SERVES 4–6

1 kg (2 lb 3 oz) sirloin beef
1 tablespoon salt
60 ml (2 fl oz/¼ cup) extra-virgin olive oil
2 rosemary sprigs
60 ml (2 fl oz/¼ cup) wine (red or white,
   or beef broth, see page 205)

Remove the beef from the fridge about 1 hour before you want to cook it. If you like, you can truss it to give it a more even shape. Rub it with the salt about 30 minutes before baking, then pat dry.

Preheat the oven to 160°C (320°F).

Pour half of the olive oil into a wide frying pan and heat over a high heat. Sear the beef all over until evenly well-browned, about 3 minutes on each side.

Grease a baking dish with the rest of the olive oil. Place the beef in the dish and thread the rosemary sprigs through the trussing (if you haven't trussed it, place them under the beef), tip over the wine (or broth) and bake until the internal temperature reaches 45°C (113°F), about 30 minutes, for rare, or 55°C (131°F), about 45 minutes, for medium-well.

Remove the beef from the oven, wrap it in aluminium foil and cover with a tea towel (dish towel) to keep warm. Let the meat rest like this for about 15 minutes (its internal temperature should rise about another 10°C (50°F) during this time) before cutting into thin slices. Serve with some of the pan juices and perhaps a side of Squashed potatoes (page 175).

Lesso Toscano e Brodo di Carne

BOILED BEEF AND BEEF BROTH

This isn't the famous *bollito* of Emilia-Romagna; this is Tuscany's rustic version, *lesso*, which literally means 'boiled'. It was prepared by Marco's great-grandmother and then his grandmother every single day. Unlike classic *bollito*, where meat is the hero, *lesso* is made for the beef broth; the meat is secondary. That isn't to say the boiled meat from *lesso* isn't appreciated – if not eaten right away, it can be put to good use in *polpette* (deep-fried, crumbed meatballs, possibly one of the world's most delicious things to make with leftovers; see page 84) and other dishes like *Francesina* (page 209), a classic Tuscan stew made with a mountain of onions.

Many classic preparations of *lesso* call for three different pieces of beef (and even half a chicken). My favourite person to ask about cuts of meat, Andrea Falaschi, a fifth-generation butcher in San Miniato, recommends a combination of sinewy cuts that have plenty of connective tissue and collagen that require long, slow cooking. His picks are a piece of *petto* (breast or brisket), *campanello* (beef hindshank, sometimes sold in a cross-cut piece as *ossobuco*) and *sorra* (shoulder or chuck). You can use a combination of these, or one or two of them.

**MAKES ABOUT 500 G
(1 LB 2 OZ) LESSO AND
2.5 LITRES (85 FL OZ/10 CUPS)
BEEF BROTH**

1 kg (2 lb 3 oz) braising beef, such as brisket,
  shank or chuck
1 onion, peeled but left whole
2 spring onions (scallions)
1 large carrot, roughly chopped
1 celery stalk, roughly chopped
2 bay leaves
3–4 sprigs flat-leaf (Italian) parsley,
  stalks and leaves
3 litres (101 fl oz/12 cups) cold water
20 g (¾ oz) sea salt

Place everything in a large stockpot and bring to a simmer over a low–medium heat. Reduce the heat to a low simmer and cover. Cook for 2 hours, then remove from the heat but leave the meat in the hot broth for 30 minutes before removing.

If eating right away, cut the meat into slices and serve warm with Squashed potatoes (page 175) or Baked onions (page 173), green salad and Salsa verde (pages 126–7). Angela's grandfather Angiolino used to enjoy it cold in the summer with sliced onion, splashed with red-wine vinegar and olive oil.

Strain the broth, discarding the vegetables and herbs. You can use this as a basic beef stock in soups and meat sugo, or cook and serve tortellini (see pages 187–8), fresh Tajarin (see pages 129–31) or other simple small pasta in it.

Polpette di Lesso

DEEP-FRIED MEATBALLS

When I make these, I have this image in my head of tiny Nonna Lina standing by the stovetop, frying, creating an enormous pyramid of these *polpette*, only to have people pop in and out of the kitchen, stealing the one on the top, too hot to even hold let alone stick in your mouth. Although I never met her (she passed away two months before I met Marco), I feel like I know her, especially when I hear the stories of her cooking.

This is probably the most delicious thing you can do with leftover meat, and it is a very Tuscan way of putting leftover boiled or roasted meat to good use. In fact, I am partial to making *lesso* (page 205) just to turn it into these meatballs. And when you have leftover *polpette* (incredibly, it happens), they are delicious cold (Marco's father, Carlo, loved them this way, and they are ideal to put in a lunchbox or take on a picnic), but Tuscans often prepare them *rifatte* (see the recipe below), which is probably the best ever dish of leftover leftovers ever invented. With each reinvention, they just keep getting better.

This makes about twenty *polpette*, which you could just as easily serve as part of an antipasto for a gathering or as a meal, with salad, for four.

MAKES APPROX. 20 POLPETTE

POLPETTE
2 medium floury potatoes
400 g (14 oz) cooked beef, such as *lesso*
 (page 205) or roasted beef
2 eggs, beaten
40 g (1½ oz) parmesan, finely grated
1 garlic clove, finely chopped
handful of flat-leaf (Italian) parsley,
 finely chopped
80 g (2¾ oz) dry breadcrumbs
vegetable oil, for frying

RIFATTE
2 tablespoons olive oil
1 garlic clove
700 g (1 lb 9 oz) tomato passata
 (puréed tomatoes)
handful of fresh herbs, such as flat-leaf
 (Italian) parsley or basil

To make the polpette, first peel and roughly chop the potatoes. Place in a saucepan of cold water and bring to the boil over a medium heat. Cook until the potatoes are easily pierced with a fork, then drain and mash with a generous pinch of salt.

Finely chop the beef (or pulse in a food processor – if you prefer a little texture like I do, go easy on the pulsing). Place in a bowl along with the mashed potato, the eggs, parmesan, garlic and parsley and combine well, adding a pinch of salt taken with three fingers and some freshly ground black pepper. Taking about 2 tablespoons of the mixture at a time, form cylindrical meatballs and place on a plate until you have used all the mixture.

Place the breadcrumbs in a shallow dish and roll each meatball to coat completely. Set aside. Pour enough vegetable oil into a wide frying pan (cast-iron is ideal for frying, if you have it) to come about 3 cm (1¼ in) of the way up and heat over a medium–high heat. The oil is ready when

a cube of bread dropped into the oil browns in 15 seconds. Fry the meatballs in a single layer for about 3 minutes on each side, or until deep brown. Drain on paper towels and salt while still hot. Serve immediately.

To make good use of any leftover meatballs, prepare a tomato sauce for 'polpette rifatte' by heating the olive oil and garlic together over a low–medium heat in a frying pan until the garlic is fragrant but not coloured, about 3–5 minutes. Add the passata and 125 ml (4 fl oz/½ cup) water, along with a three-fingered pinch of salt and some pepper. Tear over the fresh herbs and bring to a gentle simmer, cooking the sauce for about 20 minutes, uncovered. If it begins to reduce too much, add a splash more water – the sauce should be fairly liquid rather than thick, as the breaded meatballs tend to soak it up. Add the meatballs to the sauce, cover and continue cooking for 5 minutes, or until the meatballs are thoroughly warmed.

Francesina

BEEF AND ONION STEW

Lesso rifatto, or literally 'redone boiled beef', is a classic Tuscan way of recycling leftovers. Best known by the elegant name 'Francesina' (which is thought to uplift the dish's very humble appearance), it is usually done with onions but you can also find it made similarly with cardoons or potatoes as a winter dish. The idea is to use up a relatively small amount of meat and plump up the stew instead with cheap, abundant seasonal vegetables. You can adjust this recipe to the amount of leftovers you happen to have with the rule that the onions should weigh double the meat. Serve with mashed or Squashed potatoes (page 175).

SERVES 8

500 g (1 lb 2 oz) boiled meat (*lesso*, see page 205)
3 tablespoons extra-virgin olive oil
1 kg (2 lb 3 oz) red onions, sliced
½ teaspoon salt
1 sage sprig
500 ml (17 fl oz/2 cups) beef stock or water
1 x 400 g (14 oz) tin peeled tomatoes

Either slice the meat thinly, or pull it apart with forks into small chunks.

Heat the olive oil in a frying pan over a medium heat and cook the onion slices with a pinch of the salt and the sage until soft and translucent, about 20 minutes. Add a splash of the stock if you find the ingredients are getting dry or beginning to brown.

Add the tomatoes, crushing them up in the pan with a wooden spoon, then add the stock and the rest of the salt. Cook until the sauce has thickened and reduced slightly. After about 15 minutes, add the meat, taste for seasoning and continue cooking for a further 15–20 minutes. Like many stews, this is even better the next day.

209

Spiedini di Carne alla Toscana

TUSCAN-STYLE ROASTED MEAT AND BREAD SKEWERS

A heavenly and hearty roast of mixed meats, this is the sort of thing Angela might prepare for a comforting Sunday lunch, to be washed down with lots of red wine. Despite there being a delicious array of meat here, everyone is usually in agreement that the best bit is the bread. It gets crisp and golden on the edges but the inside is soft, soaked with fat from the sausages, the olive oil, a splash of wine and a hint of the herbs – it's a sponge, basically, that takes on all the flavours of the roast.

To make it work, make sure that the ingredients are threaded tightly together and, if you can, there is a piece of sausage next to at least one or two of the bread slices. If it is anything like Sunday lunch at my mother-in-law's, all you need with these is some seasonal greens, blanched and tossed through a pan with garlic and olive oil (of course I mean after you've already had a bowl of *Tortellini al sugo*, pages 186–7, and possibly a second pasta dish – and don't forget to save space for dessert).

SERVES 4

300 g (10½ oz) pork neck or fresh
    pancetta
300 g (10½ oz) pork and fennel sausages
    (approx.)
200 g (7 oz) chicken thighs
1 baguette loaf
8 fresh sage leaves
8 fresh bay leaves
80 ml (2½ fl oz/⅓ cup) extra-virgin olive oil,
    plus extra for greasing
60 ml (2 fl oz/¼ cup) dry white wine

Preheat the oven to 180°C (350°F).

Cut the pork into chunks (aim for about sixteen pieces, about 1.5–2 cm/½–¾ in thick) and divide the sausages into sixteen pieces. Cut the chicken into about eight pieces, roughly the size and thickness of the pork. Rub the pork and the chicken with a few pinches of salt and freshly ground pepper.

Cut the baguette into twenty-four rounds, about 1 cm (½ in) thick.

Thread eight metal skewers tightly with the ingredients in roughly the following order: a slice of bread, sausage, a piece of chicken, a sage leaf, a piece of pork, a slice of bread, sausage, a fresh bay leaf, a piece of pork, and finish with a slice of bread.

Place the skewers in a greased baking dish. Drizzle with the olive oil, pour the wine over the top and bake for 30 minutes, turning halfway through.

To cook this on the barbecue, after pouring the wine and olive oil over the skewers, cook over a not-too-hot part of the barbecue, turning regularly until the bread is golden and the meat is cooked through. If the bread begins to blacken too quickly I recommend finishing the cooking in the oven.

Bracioline al Burro

BEEF SCALOPPINE IN BUTTER

This is one of Marco's favourite dishes of all time, in particular for the caramel-coloured sauce that is made from the wine and butter that is to be liberally mopped up with a heaping pile of crusty bread. Nonna Lina used to prepare this for Marco when he was a child, altering the *carne ripiena* that Nonno Mario would regularly make – a thin slice of beef or veal, layered with ham and cheese, folded in half, dusted with grated parmesan and sealed with a toothpick. To this day, Marco is not a fan of meat filled with ham and cheese and Nonna Lina's simplified version without the filling was one of the only things this picky child would eat.

It became so famous in the neighbourhood that his school friends used to ask him what his nonna was making for dinner and if *bracioline al burro* was the reply, they would invite themselves over – they still, now adults with their own children, talk about this legendary dish. It is so quick and so simple, be sure to use the best quality ingredients you can find, including real (and freshly grated) parmesan.

SERVES 4

4 beef or veal scaloppine, approx. 450 g (1 lb)
80 g (2¾ oz) parmesan, finely grated
  (the best quality you can get)
100 g (3½ oz) butter
60 ml (2 fl oz/¼ cup) dry white wine
crusty bread, to serve

Rub a pinch of salt and some finely ground black pepper into each scaloppine, then thoroughly coat them in the parmesan, patting down to make sure they are well coated. In a pan, melt the butter over a medium–high heat until just beginning to colour and fry the beef slices for about 1 minute each side. Add the wine to the pan, simmer for 1 or, at the most, 2 minutes. Serve with the juices from the pan dribbled over and lots of crusty bread.

213

Rotolo di Pollo

STUFFED CHICKEN ROLL

Rolled, stuffed meat to be roasted on the stovetop has long been the classic Sunday meal for my in-laws. Often it was made with veal belly instead of chicken; sometimes there was parsley and garlic sprinkled through the middle, mortadella instead of ham, or sometimes minced (ground) meat instead of the sausage. Seasonal vegetables made their way into the stuffing too. It really depended on what was around. If you have it, you can also use home-made beef broth (see page 205) to cook the chicken in instead of water. This is our favourite combination.

You need whole, still-attached chicken breasts (preferably with fillets still attached too) for this recipe – ask your butcher to prepare the chicken breasts for this rolled roast, otherwise follow the steps below to do it yourself.

SERVES 4

500 g (1 lb 2 oz) whole, attached chicken breasts
2 eggs
1 tablespoon grated parmesan
handful of flat-leaf (Italian) parsley, chopped
80 ml (2½ fl oz/⅓ cup) olive oil
1–2 pork and fennel sausages, approx. 150 g (5½ oz)
70 g (2½ oz) ham, thinly sliced
70 g (2½ oz) provolone or fontina cheese, thinly sliced
125 ml (4 fl oz/½ cup) white wine

To prepare the chicken yourself, turn the breasts over so the smooth side is facing down. Working from the middle towards the edge, slice the breast horizontally in half, stopping as you near the edge so you can open the breast like a book. Do the same on the other side, so you now have one long piece. If you have thicker parts, you can either slice them horizontally and continue widening the chicken piece, or take a meat mallet and lightly pound the thicker parts until the chicken is evenly thick. Set aside.

Beat the eggs well with the parmesan and parsley in a small bowl. Heat half of the olive oil in a frying pan over a medium heat and gently fry the egg in a thin omelette until the top is set and the bottom is very lightly browned. Remove from the heat and set aside.

To fill the chicken, remove the casings from the sausages and spread the sausage meat all over the chicken breast. Now, layer the omelette over the top, trimming or cutting it to fit in a single layer if needed. Place the slices of ham over the omelette and finish with the cheese. Roll up the chicken tightly from one side to the other and tie well with kitchen string to help hold its shape. Rub a few pinches of salt and some freshly ground black pepper all over the chicken.

In a casserole pot, heat the rest of the olive oil over a medium–high heat. Once hot, brown the chicken evenly, about 2–3 minutes each side. Pour over the wine and cook for 1–2 minutes, simmering vigorously. Add enough water to come halfway up the chicken, bring back to a simmer, then turn the heat down to medium and cover. Cook for 15 minutes, then remove the lid, turn the chicken over and continue cooking for a further 15 minutes. Remove the chicken from the pot and rest, covered, for 10–15 minutes. During this time, increase the heat to reduce the sauce in the pot, keeping it uncovered. Serve the chicken cut into 2 cm (¾ in) thick slices with some of the sauce spooned over the top. This is perfect with some Squashed potatoes (especially the roasted version, page 175) and a salad.

Mele al Forno

BAKED APPLES

This was a highly seasonal dish when Angela was growing up – something that would be made for All Saint's Day on November 1, and make an appearance here and there throughout autumn and winter. You can still find them in the homeliest of Tuscan trattorie during these seasons, served warm, just as they are with their sugar-crusted tops and sticky bottoms. I am partial to warm, freshly baked apple cream with *Zabaione* (page 145) or even cold the next day with a blob of thick natural yoghurt.

Use a good cooking apple for this, and preferably something slightly tart (otherwise halve the sugar if using a sweet variety). Pine nuts or crumbled walnuts are also a very good addition to the filling.

SERVES 4

60 g (2 oz/½ cup) sultanas or raisins
4 medium-sized organic, unwaxed cooking
  apples
50 g (1¾ oz) butter
60 g (2 oz) sugar
splash of white wine, vin santo or rum (optional)

Preheat the oven to 180°C (350°F).

Soak the sultanas in hot water until plump, about 15 minutes. Rinse and core the apples but leave the skins on.

Lightly butter a small baking dish with half of the butter. Place the cored apples in the dish, fill the gaps with the sultanas and sprinkle the sugar over evenly. Pour about 1 cm (½ in) of water into the bottom of the pan and add a splash of wine, vin santo or rum, if desired. Bake for 30–40 minutes, or until soft and cooked through (test with a skewer), basting the apples from time to time with the liquid in the bottom of the baking dish, which will eventually turn into a delicious syrup. Let them cool slightly, then serve warm with some of the syrup dribbled over.

Torta Margherita

MARGHERITA SPONGE CAKE

Torta Margherita is made light and fluffy with starch rather than wheat flour that can take the place of sponge cake or *pan di spagna* (for example, when making *Zuppa Inglese*, page 227). It's handy for those times when you need a gluten-free dessert – or it can be enjoyed as is, simply adorned with a dusting of icing (confectioners') sugar and a good, strong coffee. The slices of pure-white coated cake are said to resemble the white petals of a daisy, lending the cake its name.

Like my favourite pastry dough recipe (see *Bocconotti* on pages 91–2), this cake is one that I first tried from Pellegrino Artusi's cookbook and have never stopped making, turning it into my own. Sometimes I add a bit of lemon or orange zest, or perhaps a bit of vanilla, but I usually keep it very simple. Over the years, it has been the cake I turn to for my daughter's birthday – two of these can be split into four layers to create an impressive, pillowy cake that, when filled with an equally pillowy frosting of Italian meringue (a soft meringue cooked over a bain-marie/double boiler), children and parents alike love (and since we seem to often have guests who can't eat dairy or wheat, this simple cake has always worked very well for everyone to enjoy).

SERVES 6–8

4 eggs
120 g (4½ oz) caster (superfine) sugar
120 g (4½ oz) potato starch, sifted (see Note)
zest of 1 lemon or 1 vanilla pod, seeds scraped
   (optional)

Preheat the oven to 180°C (350°F) and grease and line a 20 cm (8 in) round cake tin.

Separate the eggs and beat the yolks together with the sugar until very pale and creamy – like a sponge cake. The key here is to whip for much longer than you think is probably necessary (Artusi tells his nineteenth-century readers to whip for 30 minutes, though this would have been by hand). If you do want to add lemon zest or vanilla, add them now. Sift in the potato starch and carefully fold through the batter until smooth. The batter will become quite stiff.

In a separate, clean bowl, preferably glass or metal, whisk the egg whites until stiff peaks form, then delicately fold the whites through the batter, a little at a time at first, to loosen the batter. When just combined, pour into the cake tin and bake until golden on top and firm and bouncy to the touch, about 30 minutes.

NOTE

You can replace the potato starch with cornflour (cornstarch), but do not get potato starch confused with potato flour. Potato starch is light, powdery and 'squeaky' between your fingers, exactly like cornflour, whereas potato flour is simply dehydrated, cooked potato ground into flour – it is heavier and has a texture similar to wheat flour.

Torta di Mandorle di Nonna Vera

NONNA VERA'S ALMOND CAKE

This is a recipe from Marco's paternal grandmother, Nonna Vera, who is in her mid-nineties. It's a cake that my own mother-in-law, Angela, has made countless times, even inventing a summer version where she leaves off the almonds and instead tops the cooked cake with fresh strawberries macerated in sugar and whipped cream – she thinks of this almond cake as decidedly wintry, but I like it at any moment especially with an espresso.

It's a solid, foolproof recipe, easy to remember and so easy to whip up – all you need is a bowl and a fork. Practical, just like Nonna Vera.

SERVES 6–8

150 g (5½ oz/1 cup) plain (all-purpose) flour
150 g (5½ oz) sugar
150 g (5½ oz) butter, melted
1 whole egg
3 egg yolks
finely grated zest of 1 lemon
100 g (3½ oz) blanched whole almonds
icing (confectioners') sugar, to serve

Combine the flour and sugar in a bowl. Pour over the melted butter and mix. Add the egg and yolks one at a time, and then the lemon zest, stirring with a fork.

Preheat the oven to 180°C (350°F) and grease and line a 20 cm (8 in) round cake tin. Pour the cake batter into the tin and top with the whole almonds, pushing them in slightly.

Bake for 30 minutes, or until golden brown on top. Dust with icing sugar to serve.

219

THE COOKBOOK THAT TAUGHT ME ABOUT ITALIAN HOME COOKING

My favourite cookbook for traditional Tuscan recipes was written in 1891 – Pellegrino Artusi's *Scienza in Cucina e l'Arte di Mangiare Bene* (*Science in the Kitchen and the Art of Eating Well*, affectionately known simply as 'Artusi' to Italians). I was introduced to it by the tattered copy with yellowing pages belonging to Nonna Lina that sits in Angela's kitchen. The splattered cover is falling off and the book opens instantly to the most well-used pages where the spine has cracked from overuse – namely, recipe no. 589 (of 790), three shortcrust pastry recipes with Nonna Lina's handwriting pointing to 'recipe B' (my favourite too).

I was immediately hooked. I loved that so many of his recipes felt familiar to me – he himself moved to Florence from his native Emilia-Romagna in the early 1850s and lived there until his death in 1910. Cooking from Artusi was like eating at my favourite old trattorie in Florence or at my mother-in-law's for Sunday lunch.

My relationship with Artusi deepened in January 2011 when my blog was just a month old. I decided to begin a series featuring one of his recipes a month for a year, choosing recipes from his seasonal menus (like the ones on page 242) or, with eyes closed, letting fate pick a recipe for me. The book accompanied me everywhere, nestled in my handbag or on my bedside table, and I got to know Artusi very well.

Artusi's recipes aren't written in a way that we are used to today. Many specific directions are often left out, the assumption being that the nineteenth-century reader knows what to do or understands what 'enough' means when the instruction is to add 'enough' rice to the minestrone. Cooking times and heat temperatures are rare (just as well, since baking in Artusi's time would have been done in a cast-iron cooking range or a wood-fired oven). There are no pictures, aside from a handful of simple diagrams. But despite this, I find Artusi still current, as if the recipes have been unaffected by time, as if your great-grandmother is in the kitchen cooking with you.

The story behind the cookbook, a labour of love, is inspiring. Seventy-one-year-old Artusi, a businessman with an enormous passion for cooking, could not find anyone to publish his book so he decided to self-publish it, initially printing only 1,000 copies. Before long, it was one of the books that every single Italian household had a copy of (and still does), along with Pinocchio and other best-known Italian classics. Today, Artusi is still a household name and he is known as the grandfather of Italian cuisine thanks to his book – the first definitive collection of recipes of the newly unified nation of Italy.

Torta di Mele di Angela

ANGELA'S APPLE CAKE

My mother-in-law, Angela, has a 'recipe book': a large hardcover agenda from 1981 where she writes down recipes she likes or wants to try. They're scattered randomly, scrawled on the days of the week where you would normally record birthdays, appointments and reminders. It's rather impractical because you have to flick through 365 days to find the scribbled recipe you're looking for, but she has been using it diligently for nearly forty years. This apple cake was the first recipe she wrote down in it, and although she doesn't remember anymore where it came from, it was one that she made often when Marco was a child.

I love it because it's quite different from the usual Tuscan apple cake, which is a simple cake topped with a single layer of sliced apples. I suspect this version is not even Tuscan at all, as it requires quite a good amount of butter. The cake on the bottom is rather dense and crumbly – a support for all the apples that melt down into a surprisingly thin layer, topped with a veil of butter and sugar. It's absolutely delicious just out of the oven, still warm, and I would say always does better with a bit of warming up even the next day or so. The fact that Angela calls this cake '*la torta di mele e panna*' – the cake with apple and cream – to distinguish it from a regular apple cake tells you that you should always serve this with freshly whipped cream.

SERVES 8

250 ml (8½ fl oz/1 cup) freshly whipped cream,
   to serve

CAKE

200 g (7 oz) butter, softened, plus extra
   for greasing
60 g (2 oz) sugar
1 egg
150 g (5½ oz/1 cup) plain (all-purpose) flour
2 teaspoons baking powder
zest and juice of 1 lemon
650 g (1 lb 7 oz) (about 4) apples, peeled
   and sliced
splash of brandy or rum

TOPPING

80 g (2¾ oz) butter, softened
80 g (2/34 oz/⅓ cup) sugar
50 g (1¾ oz/⅓ cup) plain (all-purpose) flour

Preheat the oven to 180°C (350°F) and grease and line a 20 cm (8 in) round cake tin.

For the cake, combine the butter, sugar, egg, flour, baking powder, lemon zest and juice and a pinch of salt until creamy. Press into the prepared cake tin. Layer over the apple slices and sprinkle them with brandy.

For the topping, rub or mix together the butter, sugar and flour in a bowl. Top the apples with this mixture and place in the oven. Bake for 30 minutes, or until the top is golden brown and the apples have cooked down and become tender.

Allow to cool (or eat warm, my preference) and serve with some softly whipped cream.

Torta di Nonno Mario

NONNO MARIO'S CAKE

This is a cake for family celebrations – the cake that Nonno Mario would always make for birthdays, holidays and other special occasions, only substituting it in the summer for its similar cousin, *Zuppa Inglese* (pages 227), which has basically all the same elements other than the sponge and, being chilled, made a nice dessert for the warm weather. Nonna Lina called it '*gattò*' (*gateau*); Angela calls it '*la torta traballosa*', 'wobbly cake', because Mario would put it together with warm pastry cream between the layers, which were not evenly sliced so it would lean and totter a little. There is a very similar dessert in Abruzzo known as *pizza dolce*, and Italian-Americans would recognise it as 'Italian rum cake', while Italian-Australians call it 'continental cake'. But for us, it's simply 'Mario's cake'.

SERVES 8–10

butter, for greasing

PAN DI SPAGNA (SPONGE)
120 g (4½ oz) plain (all-purpose) flour
30 g (1 oz/¼ cup) cornflour (cornstarch)
   or potato starch (see Note, page 218)
4 eggs, at room temperature
120 g (4½ oz) sugar

SYRUP
2 tablespoons Alchermes or rum (see Notes,
   page 226)
30 g (1 oz) sugar
80 ml (2½ fl oz/⅓ cup) water
rind of 1 lemon (optional)

PASTRY CREAM
500 ml (17 fl oz/2 cups) full-cream (whole) milk
4 egg yolks
120 g (4½ oz) sugar
30 g (1 oz/¼ cup) cornflour (cornstarch)
scraped seeds of 1 vanilla bean or zest
   of 1 lemon
60 g (2 oz) dark chocolate, chopped

DECORATION
250 ml (8½ fl oz/1 cup) pouring (single/light)
   cream, whipped
1 tablespoon cornflour (cornstarch)
3 tablespoons icing (confectioners') sugar
100 g (3½ oz) slivered almonds
   (optional; see Notes, page 226)

Preheat the oven to 180°C (350°F) and grease and line a 22 cm (8¾ in) round cake tin.

To make the pan di spagna, sift the flours together into a bowl. In a separate bowl, whisk the eggs and sugar together for about 10 minutes until very creamy, pale, thick and pillowy. Fold in the flours very gently and pour into the cake tin.

Bake for 35 minutes, or until golden brown and springy on top. A toothpick inserted in the middle of the cake should come out clean. Remove from the tin and leave to cool completely (even better if you made it the night before and refrigerated it overnight) before slicing into three even discs about 2 cm (¾ in) thick.

To make the syrup, combine all the ingredients in a small saucepan and bring to the boil. Simmer for 5 minutes, then take off the heat and set aside until needed.

To make the pastry cream, heat the milk in a saucepan until steaming but not boiling. In a heatproof bowl, whisk the yolks and sugar until smooth. Add the cornflour, vanilla or lemon and then the milk, a little bit at first, then combining the rest. Place the bowl in a bain-marie (double boiler) over a saucepan of simmering water over a low heat and whisk steadily until thickened, about 12–15 minutes (it will thicken quite suddenly, so pay close attention to the point when you see it begin to change).

224

Divide between two bowls and, in one, stir through the dark chocolate until melted and smooth. Leave to cool completely.

Assemble the cake by placing the bottom disc of cake on a flat plate or cake stand. Brush generously with the syrup. Smooth over the chocolate pastry cream. Place the middle layer of sponge on top. Brush again with the syrup, then smooth over the plain pastry cream. Place the final layer of cake on top. If serving the cake the next day, wrap well in plastic wrap until needed.

The day you plan to serve it, prepare the whipped cream: place the cream, cornflour and sugar in a bowl and whisk until you just arrive at firm peaks. Cover the sides and top of the cake with the cream. If you want to, decorate with some slivered almonds. Serve in thin slices.

NOTES

If you would like to make this wheat-free, use the Torta Margherita (page 218) recipe in place of this sponge.

The pan di spagna, syrup and pastry creams can both be made up to a few days in advance, and the cake is best when put together the day before you want to serve it; it makes it a little more stable and less 'traballosa'. Although Mario didn't decorate his cake with anything other than whipped cream, you could add crushed nuts, shaved chocolate or some fresh berries. Sometimes, instead of the whipped cream, Mario would cover the cake with warm, liquid chocolate that would drip down the sides.

If you don't like Alchermes – some aunts and cousins in the family don't – you can use rum instead, or replace the syrup entirely with strong espresso.

Zuppa Inglese

This is a classic Tuscan celebratory dessert. The apricot jam is not common these days, but it is included in Artusi's recipe and I've always liked the contrasting tart flavour it gives and the colour it adds. If you want to make a non-alcoholic version, use simply the sugar syrup without the Alchermes and rum, or you can use coffee instead. If you don't have a deep glass bowl – at least 10 cm (4 in) deep and 22 cm (8¾ in) in diameter, but you can easily go a bit bigger – you can also use a large rectangular glass dish.

SERVES 8–10

PASTRY CREAM
8 egg yolks
170 g (6 oz/¾ cup) caster (superfine) sugar
80 g (2¾ oz) cornflour (cornstarch)
½ vanilla bean, seeds scraped
1 litre (34 fl oz/4 cups) full-cream (whole) milk, warmed
100 g (3½ oz) dark chocolate, finely chopped

TO ASSEMBLE
2 tablespoons sugar
50 ml (1¾ fl oz) rum
125 ml (4 fl oz/½ cup) Alchermes
400 g (14 oz) savoiardi biscuits
100 g (3½ oz) apricot jam
250 ml (8½ fl oz/1 cup) single (pouring) cream, whipped, to serve
bittersweet cocoa powder, to serve (optional)

To make the pastry creams, whisk the yolks and sugar until smooth in a heatproof bowl. Add the cornflour, vanilla seeds and then the milk, a little bit at first, then combining the rest. Place the bowl in a bain-marie (double boiler) over a saucepan of simmering water on a low heat and whisk steadily until thickened, about 12–15 minutes (it will thicken quite suddenly, so pay close attention to the point when you see it begin to change).

Set aside roughly two-thirds of the pastry cream in a shallow bowl to cool it quickly, giving it a stir every now and then so that a skin doesn't form (if making this well in advance, cover with plastic wrap that touches the top of the pastry cream and store in the fridge). Stir the chocolate into the rest of the still-hot pastry cream, mixing until smooth. Set aside to cool.

Prepare a syrup by dissolving the sugar in 125 ml (4 fl oz/½ cup) water in a small saucepan and allowing to simmer for about 5 minutes. Add the rum and Alchermes and continue simmering for another 5 minutes (if you like it boozy, let the syrup cool before stirring in the alcohol).

Dip the savoiardi on both sides into the Alchermes mixture and place the biscuits side by side to cover the bottom of a glass serving bowl.

Cover the savoiardi with a layer apricot jam, then half of the plain pastry cream. Add another layer of Alchermes-dipped savoiardi, followed by a layer of the chocolate pastry cream, another layer of dipped savoidari and the rest of the plain pastry cream.

If you have the space, you can add an extra layer of dipped savoiardi, then cover and chill in the fridge for at least 2 hours (or overnight) before topping with freshly whipped cream just before serving. Alternatively, leave off the top layer of savoiardi and chill the zuppa inglese as described. Before serving, dust with cocoa powder (if using) and serve with the cream on the side.

NOTE

This is often made with sponge cake cut into thin slices and then fingers – savoiardi biscuits are, after all, simply sponge cake made into dry biscuits. If you want to try the sponge, use the recipe for Mario's cake (pages 224–6) and, if you want a wheat-free version, you can also use the recipe for Torta Margherita (page 218).

227

ZUPPA INGLESE – ENGLISH OR ITALIAN?

The origins of *zuppa Inglese* are well-debated, with a history that is hard to untangle because of so little first-hand documentation and so many fanciful legends. It's a simple, old-fashioned, sometimes gaudy yet much-loved dessert made of layers of chocolate cream and pastry cream, sporting the bright pink hue of Alchermes-soaked savoiardi (sponge fingers or lady finger biscuits).

The similarity to British trifle is so striking that the literal translation of its name, 'English soup', probably comes as no surprise. In *Italian Food*, Elizabeth David calls it a 'trifle much glorified' and, indeed, many even assume that *zuppa Inglese* is an English dessert – an Italianised trifle – brought over by English expatriates living in Florence in the nineteenth century. But I'm with those that insist that it is an age-old Italian preparation simply named in honour of the English.

One theory on the origin of the dessert's name comes from the use of the *crema inglese* (literally 'English cream', otherwise known as *creme anglais* or pouring custard, which is made without any starch or flour). In Pellegrino Artusi's 1891 recipe for *zuppa Inglese*, he cites it is a Tuscan dessert, saying that the delicate *crema inglese* that the Tuscans like to use is too runny for his liking so he uses *crema pasticcera*, pastry cream, thickened with starch, which is how it's usually made today.

Interestingly, Artusi makes no reference to it being of British origin, which he does with the many English recipes included in his cookbook, such as *Lesso all'inglese* (Toad in the hole), *Mele all'inglese* (English-style apples, a sort of apple pie) and *Quattro-quarti all'inglese* (Currant-studded pound cake). You'll notice the English recipes are usually designated by the '*all'inglese*' in their title – in the English style.

The fascinating account of long-term British expatriate Gladys Gretton, *The Englishwoman in Italy*, written in 1860, mentions *zuppa Inglese* as a regional specialty of Le Marche. Gretton attended a typical peasant wedding in Ancona and describes everything in enormous detail, paying particular attention to differences between British and Italian culture. She seems almost amused to note that the *zuppa Inglese* is named after the national British fondness for alcohol and makes no hint of it being anything but a local dessert: 'Sweet dishes they do not seem to care for, excepting sometimes *zuppa Inglese* – sponge cakes, soaked in rum, and covered with custard, so named in compliment to our national taste for ardent spirits, supposed indispensable to a Briton's daily refection.'

While English trifle first appears in Thomas Dawson's cookbooks of 1585, in *The Oxford Companion to Food* Alan Davidson points out that there is a recipe of this name in Cristoforo di Messisbugo's recipe book (published posthumously in 1557), even if Messisbugo's *zuppa magra Inglese* is a rather different preparation: stewed parsley roots in an egg-thickened bouillon broth poured over slices of bread and sprinkled with cinnamon and sugar. The word 'zuppa' (soup) here is more like the English word 'sop', referring to bread soaking in liquid, which explains how this dessert is also considered a 'zuppa' – not a soup, but a dish made of sponge soaked in an alcoholic syrup.

There is another (perhaps far-fetched) legend that dates the *zuppa Inglese* to sixteenth-century Tuscany, where it was served to Duke Cosimo I de' Medici in 1552 in Siena and became known as 'zuppa del Duca', the Duke's soup.

Perhaps it's not that one dessert evolved from the other, but that they are quite separate desserts that are simply similar – after all, dipping sponge or biscuits into alcohol and topping it with custard is a mouth-watering but not entirely original idea. Gillian Riley in the *Oxford Companion to Italian Food* agrees that *zuppa Inglese* is unlikely to have been of English origin, saying, 'From dunking cake or biscuits in a dessert wine, it was but a short step to layering them in a dish, soaked in wine, liqueurs, or fruit and dousing them with custard or cream'. And this is probably the best explanation of the evolution of this Italian classic.

Budino di Riso

BAKED RICE PUDDING

This delicious, rustic and homely baked rice pudding comes right out of Pellegrino Artusi's classic cookbook, with a few modifications. It was a constant when Angela was growing up, often served with their own family variation of warm, liquid chocolate (*Sanguinaccio al cioccolato*, page 96) spooned over the top. I can't help but think of it as bread and butter pudding made with rice instead; it tastes remarkably similar.

It is best eaten warm, when it has not long been out of the oven. It doesn't keep well for longer than a day or two as the rice tends to harden. So, although it's usually made in one large baking dish, if you're serving fewer people, you can halve this quantity and bake it in individual ramekins.

SERVES 8–10

160 g (5½ oz) short-grain rice, such as arborio
750 ml (25½ fl oz/3 cups) full-cream (whole) milk, or as needed
100 g (3½ oz) sugar
½ vanilla bean, seeds scraped
zest of 1 lemon
40 g (1½ oz) butter, plus extra for greasing
100 g (3½ oz) raisins
2 whole eggs
2 egg yolks
splash of rum, cognac or vin santo (optional)
1 tablespoon breadcrumbs

Combine the rice with the milk in a saucepan and bring to a simmer with a pinch of salt. After 10 minutes, add the sugar, vanilla seeds, lemon zest and butter, and continue cooking over a low–medium heat for 30 minutes, or until the rice is very soft and the milk is almost all absorbed (if you notice the rice is absorbing the milk too quickly, add more milk – up to another 250 ml/8½ fl oz/1 cup – until the rice is cooked). Remove from the heat.

Preheat the oven to 180°C (350°F).

When the rice mixture has cooled slightly but is still hot, add the raisins, eggs, yolks and rum, and stir well.

Grease a solid 25 cm (10 in) round cake tin or similar-sized baking dish with butter and scatter over breadcrumbs to coat all sides. Pour the rice mixture into the tin or dish and bake for 20 minutes, or until the top is golden brown.

233

Frittelle di ciliegie

CHERRY FRITTERS

Not far from San Miniato is another pretty hilltop town of the Pisan countryside called Lari, where cherries have been cultivated for centuries. Once a year, on the verge of summer, nearly twenty native varieties of cherry can be sampled at the town's cherry festival (one of Tuscany's oldest *sagre*, or food festivals). At the festival's market you can find not only fresh cherries, piled high in baskets, but also cherry delicacies, from pies to liqueurs to jams in various shades of scarlet – there's even cherry-scented beer. But, by far, the most popular attraction is the stall where a team of nonne in their aprons diligently whip up a paddling pool–sized bowl of batter and deep-fry fresh cherry fritters in an equally giant pot of bubbling oil. The line is long, but it's worth the wait for a paper cone full of piping hot, sugar-crusted fritters. This is how I recreate them at home.

234

MAKES ABOUT 24 FRITTERS

200 g (7 oz/1⅓ cups) plain (all-purpose) flour
3 teaspoons baking powder
120 g (4½ oz) sugar
zest of 1 lemon
1 egg
180 ml (6 fl oz) full-cream (whole) milk
splash of Alchermes or rum (optional)
200 g (7 oz) fresh cherries, pitted and
    roughly chopped
vegetable oil, for frying

Place the flour, baking powder, 2 tablespoons of the sugar, the lemon zest and a pinch of salt in a mixing bowl. Stir together briefly, then add the egg and milk, whisking until you have a smooth batter, rather like pancake batter. Add a splash of Alchermes, if using, and stir through the cherries.

Place the rest of the sugar in a small bowl (I prefer something shallow).

Pour enough oil into a small–medium saucepan so that the fritters can float. Heat over a medium heat to 160°C (320°F), or until a cube of white bread dropped into the oil turns golden brown in about 15 seconds.

Give the batter a stir in case the cherry pieces have fallen to the bottom, then drop a tablespoon of batter into the hot oil and fry evenly, turning to cover all sides, until deep golden brown, about 2½–3 minutes (see Note). They will puff-up into walnut-sized fritters. Aim to cook several at a time, in batches. Transfer the cooked fritters to a wire rack lined with paper towels to drain the excess oil for a moment before rolling the fritters, still hot, in the sugar. These are best eaten warm, right away.

NOTE

These fritters should be fried rather slowly so that they cook all the way through – if the temperature is too high, they will brown too quickly and remain raw inside. I suggest sacrificing the first one or two fritters by looking inside to ensure they are cooked through to the centre. Once you have the temperature stabilised and the timing right, frying these fritters is a cinch. It is a good idea to scoop out any little drops of batter that have fallen into the oil before they burn, and to replenish the oil about halfway through.

Zuccherini

ANISEED BISCUITS

Nonna Maria, Angela's maternal grandmother, was responsible for the baked goods at the alimentari and bar that she and her husband, Angiolino, ran in the middle of town. She was a sturdy country woman with the arms of someone who doesn't complain one bit about stirring a giant pot of polenta for an hour until her face is red, breaking chicken necks, or plucking little black birds while everyone else looks away.

Her *zuccherini* were well known, so much so that not only did they become the one and only true specialty of the town of Fucecchio, but the only bakery that still produces them today, every carnival season in February, uses her recipe. The large, sweet, blonde rings of aniseed-flavoured biscuit were traditionally strung on a pole to hang in the pantry and were meant to last until Lent. As they are baked for a short time, they retain quite a soft, crumbly interior. They're quite perfect broken off into small pieces to dip into coffee.

MAKES 8 LARGE ZUCCHERINI

350 g (12½ oz/2⅓ cups) plain (all-purpose)
  flour, plus extra for dusting
1½ teaspoons baking powder
200 g (7 oz) sugar
2 teaspoons aniseeds
2 whole eggs
1 tablespoon honey
zest of 1 lemon
1½ tablespoons sassolino, sambuca or other
  aniseed-flavoured liqueur (or milk)

Preheat the oven to 180°C (350°F).

Combine the dry ingredients in a bowl, make a little well in the middle and crack in the eggs, adding the honey, lemon zest and alcohol. Begin mixing the eggs into the dry ingredients with a fork at first, then you will have to use your hands to bring it together to a soft dough. Wrap in plastic wrap and chill the dough in the fridge for about 30 minutes.

On a lightly floured surface, divide the dough into two pieces and, working one piece at a time, roll the dough into a long log, about 2.5 cm (1 in) thick. Cut into lengths about 22 cm (8¾ in) long and join the ends together to produce large rings. Transfer them to a baking sheet lined with baking paper (leave plenty of room between the biscuits as they will expand) and, with a sharp knife, make fairly deep, decorative indentations across the surface of the biscuits. Continue with the rest of the dough.

Place the baking sheets in the middle rack of the oven and bake for 12–15 minutes, or until the biscuits are only very lightly browned on the top and bottom. They will still feel slightly soft when you take them out of the oven, but will harden a little as they cool. They will last a long time stored in a cool, dry place in an airtight container.

THE LOST RECIPE

I was dropping in on Marco's aunt and uncle, Franca and Riccardo. We let ourselves in through the gate, attempting not to let Asia, the giant Maremma sheepdog, escape, and slipped into the house where, behind a pile of books, Riccardo, a journalist now in his late seventies, was printing out a short story to share with me. It's about cake – he thought I would like it.

It was a cake often made by Nonna Maria, a farmer's daughter from the countryside near Pisa, and a baker. The cake pervades Riccardo's memory like a ghost. He remembers the smell, the taste, the month of the year – she made it in November, a month of cold, short, rainy days, during a festive season when the fair would come to town. He remembers it as '*una bomba*' – of calories, that is. It's very dense, short cake, heavy with eggs and lard (olive oil and butter were luxuries). It was eaten around the fire, one piece devoured after another.

Riccardo has spent years searching for this recipe, based entirely on the memory of eating it when he was young. At first, we thought it might be like a sort of Florentine *schiacciata*: a fluffy, yeasted cake typical of Florence, made exclusively during the carnival period in February (already that raised my doubts), heady with the aromas of orange zest and vanilla and enriched with lard. I made it for him to try, but it was too fluffy, too perfumed, too dainty with its veil of icing sugar and cocoa powder, to be the one.

'It's more rustic,' Riccardo said.

'And denser, much denser,' Franca piped up.

They got married when they were both seventeen years old. They have been together for more than sixty years and have three great-grandchildren. Even Franca remembers this cake. In fact, although it's Riccardo's memory, Franca is a great cook, and she knows cakes, so I listen to her recollection of it too and, in particular, to a detail that Riccardo doesn't mention.

'There were *ciccioli* in it,' she assures me, speaking of savoury, crunchy, porky bits scattered throughout the cake.

Ciccioli lend crunch to the cake. Similar to pork scratchings, they can be eaten as is as a rather addictive snack, but they're more traditionally found sprinkled through polenta, bread or, in this case, cake.

I didn't have to look very far for inspiration – Pellegrino Artusi has a recipe in his nineteenth-century cookbook for *focaccia coi siccioli* (*ciccioli*). And although he calls it a focaccia, it's not a bread but actually a sweet, very dense, flat cake. It's a country cake that has a comforting, satisfying quality worthy of cherishing as a memory for a lifetime.

Clockwise from top From left: Mario, Angela, Mario's brother Carlo with his children, Giorgio and Paola; kneeling in front are Lina, Franca holding baby Lorella, and Riccardo; Nonna Maria with baby Riccardo; Nonna Maria

Torta con i Ciccioli di Nonna Maria

NONNA MARIA'S LARD CAKE

Nonna Maria was from the countryside and was known for her no-nonsense baked goods, such as *Zuccherini* (page 237) and this dense cake enriched with lard and *ciccioli*. *Ciccioli* are small, dry pieces of fatty pork, cooked slowly until dry and all the fat has melted out of them – this part is then drained for making lard. They are similar to pork scratchings and are, at times, spiced or salted, but at their simplest, left plain and unseasoned. It may sound strange, but the sweet-savoury result is much like the wonderful effect of having pancakes with maple syrup and crispy bacon, though much subtler.

SERVES 8

200 g (7 oz) sugar
150 g (5½ oz) softened butter
60 g (2 oz/1/4 cup) softened lard
2 whole eggs
2 egg yolks
500 g (1 lb 2 oz) plain (all-purpose) flour
60 ml (2 fl oz/¼ cup) vin santo (or white wine, rum or Marsala)
zest of 1 lemon or orange
150 g (5½ oz) *ciccioli* (unseasoned, deep-fried pork fat pieces), finely chopped
icing (confectioners') sugar, for serving

Cream together the sugar, butter and lard in a bowl. Add the eggs and yolks, one at a time, until well incorporated. Mix in the flour and, once smooth, the wine, followed by the citrus zest and the ciccioli pieces. Stir until just combined.

Spread out the mixture in a rectangular tin (such as a brownie tin) lined with baking paper. Bake at 180°C (350°F) for approximately 45 minutes, or until deep golden brown on top and springy in the middle. Cut into squares and serve dusted with icing sugar.

MENUS

I have always loved menu suggestions in cookbooks. Pellegrino Artusi has a section at the back of his famous cookbook *La Scienza in Cucina e l'Arte di Mangiar Bene*, titled *Note di Pranzi*, 'Notes on Meals', where he includes two menus for each month of the year with suggestions from the nearly 800 recipes in his book. The very first recipe in the very first menu under the heading 'January' happens to be tortellini.

When my mother-in-law Angela (and even Marco) was growing up, there was a ritual to meals: holidays were celebrated with the same menu year after year; weekday meals looked the same with very little variation, day in, day out, changing only with the seasons, while special dishes were reserved for Sundays. This means that *cotolette di agnello* always taste like Easter, chestnuts roasted in a perforated pan are a reminder of cold autumn nights, and tortellini are comforting, warming and special all at once.

NEW YEAR'S DAY

Tortellini al sugo (Tortellini with meat sauce) 186–7
Brasato al barolo (Beef braised in red wine) 136–7
Patate schiacciate (Squashed potatoes) 174
Torta di Nonno Mario (Mario's cake) 224–5

EASTER SUNDAY

Pinzimonio (Raw vegetables for antipasto) 166
Tortellini al sugo (Tortellini with meat sauce) 186–7
Cotolette d'agnello fritte (Deep-fried lamb chops) 202
Carciofi fritti (Deep-fried battered artichokes) 169
Zuppa Inglese 227

PRIMO MAGGIO (LABOUR DAY), 1 MAY

Insalata Russa (Russian salad) 171
Pomarola di Nonna Lina (Nonna Lina's fresh Tuscan tomato sauce) 176–7
Rotolo di pollo (Stuffed chicken roll) 214
Patate schiacciate e piselli (Squashed potatoes – 175 – and fresh peas)
Fragole con lo zucchero (Strawberries sprinkled with sugar)

FERRAGOSTO, 15 AUGUST

Pasta con pomodoro crudo (Pasta with raw tomato sauce) 178
Parmigiana alle melanzane (Eggplant parmigiana) 50
Bistecca (Florentine-style steak)
Peperoni arrostiti (Grilled capsicums) 47
Macedonia (Fruit salad)

TUTTI I SANTI (ALL SAINT'S DAY), 1 NOVEMBER

Pasta al forno di Angela (Angela's lasagne) 180–3
Spit roast
Cipolle al forno (Baked onions) 173
Mele al forno (Baked apples) 216
Castagne (Roast chestnuts)

CHRISTMAS DAY

Tartine e insalata russa (Tartines and Russian salad) 113 & 171
Tortellini in brodo (Tortellini in broth)
Pasta al forno di Angela (Angela's lasagne) 180–3
Roast beef all'inglese (English-style roast beef) 204
Spiedini di carne alla toscana (Tuscan-style roasted meat and bread skewers) 210
Torta di Nonno Mario (Mario's cake) 224–6
Frutta secca (Dried fruit and nuts)

NEW YEAR'S EVE

Tartine e pinzimonio (Tartines and Raw vegetables for antipasto) 113 & 166
Tortellini al sugo (Tortellini with meat sauce) 186–7
Fegatelli e rapini (Roast pork liver and cime di rapa)
Pandoro e zabaione (Pandoro slices served with zabaione) 145

244

REFERENCES

These are the books I use regularly and have referred to,
some in Italian and some in English. I list them here for further
recipes and stories about the traditional, home-style cuisine
of Taranto, Turin and Tuscany.

Artusi, Pellegrino 1960, *La Scienza in Cucina e l'Arte di Mangiar Bene*,
Giunti Marzocco, Firenze.

Attorre, Antonio 2000, *Ricette di Osterie di Puglia: Mare, Erbe, Fornelli*,
Slow Food Editore, Bra.

Boni, Ada 1999, *Il Talismano della Felicità*, Editore Colombo, Roma.

Cardellicchio, Riccardo 2009, *Il Pozzo di Muscioro e Altre Storie Fucecchiesi*,
Edizione dell'Erba, Fucecchio.

David, Elizabeth 2011, *Italian Food*, revised edition, Penguin, London.

Field, Carol 1985, *The Italian Baker*, reissue edition, Harper & Rowe, New York.

Gray, Patience 2009, *Honey from a Weed: Fasting and Feasting in Tuscany,
Catalonia, The Cyclades and Apulia*, Prospect Books, London.

Lodi, Beppe and De Giacomi, Luciano 1999, *Nonna Genia*, Araba Fenice, Boves.

Petroni, Paolo 2009, *Il Libro della Vera Cucina Toscana*, Giunti Editore, Firenze.

Risolvo, Rosa and Enzo 2014, *Mange e Bbive Tarandine: Storia Sapori e Saperi
della Cucina Tradizionale Tarantina e Pugliese*, Scorpione Editrice, Taranto.

Ross, Janet 2015, *The Land of Manfred, Prince of Tarentum and King of Sicily:
Rambles in Remote Parts of Southern Italy, With Special Reference to Their
Historical Associations*, Forgotten Books, London.

Servi, Edda Machlin 1981, *The Classic Cuisine of the Italian Jews:
Traditional Recipes and Menus and a Memoir of a Vanished Way of Life*,
Everest House, New York.

INDEX

246

249

GRAZIE

This book, like my other cookbooks, could not have been dreamt up and realised without the encouragement and support of my husband, Marco, who cooks, cleans, edits, inspires, does the shopping, the driving, the nappy changing and more. Grazie, amore mio, for everything; I hope this is something that you and our darling daughters, Mariù and Luna, will be able to treasure. You are all part of every book I write, but especially this one.

It could not have been made more beautiful thanks to the work of the incredible team of people that made this happen. Thank you to the entire Hardie Grant team, especially to Jane, for your constant support and for believing this was a story worth telling, to Loran for making it such a smooth journey and to Andrea for keeping me on my toes.

To the ever-inspiring women who I have been so fortunate to work with again and again. To Deb and Lauren, who came all the way to Tuscany during the sweltering summer to style and photograph the recipes, you are incredible. Thank you for bringing the recipes to life through your craft with a reassuring and zen-like attitude and for the laughs over buckets of spritz. To the most clever Allison, thank you again for designing a book that simply blows me away. And to Alice and Helen, thank you for your dedication and for squeezing into a tiny, unlikely kitchen.

Thank you to all the friends and family who gave me advice, encouragement and inspiration along the way – I had been talking about the bones of this book for a while. To Tessa Kiros, especially, not only for agreeing to write a foreword or because your cookbooks have been an inspiration for me since day one, but also because one day over coffee in Florence, you gave me some advice that I will always remember and that encouraged me to pitch the idea for this book. Thank you from the bottom of my heart.

To my own family in Australia, thank you for sharing in these stories and recipes from long distance. Also to my clever sister, Hana Davies, thank you for editing my photographs and making them shine.

To Irene Berni and Paolo Moretti, Giovanni Berni and Graziella Bartalesi, thank you for letting us into your beautiful Tuscan home and for allowing us to make Valdirose ours for a moment. Such a special place.

To Alice Adams, Tobias Brown, Rachel Lewis, Louisa Loring, Morgan Maher, Deborah Manz, Susan McCreight, Emma Olson, Kirsteen Travers and Joanna Troha, a huge thank you for your enthusiastic recipe testing and for helping give me the confidence to send these recipes out into the world!

Finally, to Angela and Riccardo, thank you for sharing your stories and your recipes with me over the years. I hope I have done them, along with the stories of your family, justice. Grazie per aver condiviso le vostre storie e ricette con me, questo libro è dedicato a voi.

ABOUT THE AUTHOR

Born in Australia to a Japanese mother and an Australian father, Emiko Davies has spent most of her life living abroad – after an adolescence in China, she gained a university degree in the United States and now, for more than a decade, she has called Italy home.

She fell in love with Florence as a twenty-something art restoration student, soaking in the Florentine lifestyle and learning Italian along the way. Then she met Marco, a sommelier, who shares her lifelong passion for cooking and travelling. In 2010 Emiko began a dream project — a food blog sprinkled with her own photographs, where she could tell the true stories behind regional and historical Italian dishes from the point of view of a foreigner living in Italy. She soon caught the eye of Food52 co-founder Amanda Hesser who called her a 'Renaissance woman for the internet era'.

Emiko continues to develop recipes and write about food and travel for Food52, as well as contributing to publications such as Italian newspaper *Corriere della Sera*, *The Guardian*, *Gourmet Traveller*, *Conde Nast Traveller* and more. This is her third cookbook after *Florentine* and *Acquacotta*, which was shortlisted for the Fortnum & Mason Award for Best Cookery Book. Emiko lives in Florence with her husband, Marco, and their two daughters.

Published in 2019 by Hardie Grant Books,
an imprint of Hardie Grant Publishing

Hardie Grant Books (Melbourne)
Building 1, 658 Church Street
Richmond, Victoria 3121

Hardie Grant Books (London)
5th & 6th Floors
52–54 Southwark Street
London SE1 1UN
hardiegrantbooks.com

A catalogue record for this
book is available from the
National Library of Australia

Tortellini at Midnight
ISBN 978 1 74379 453 1

10 9 8 7 6 5 4 3 2 1

Publishing Director: Jane Willson
Project Editor: Loran McDougall
Editor: Andrea O'Connor @ Asterisk & Octopus
Design Manager: Jessica Lowe
Designer: Allison Colpoys
Food Photographer: Lauren Bamford
Food Stylist: Deb Kaloper
Home Economist: Alice Adams
Production Manager: Todd Rechner

Colour reproduction by Splitting Image Colour Studio
Printed in China by 1010 Printing International Limited